100 Fine Motor Ideas

volume 2 of Fine Motor Ideas

Also in this series:

99 Fine Motor Ideas

100 Fine Motor Ideas --- Toys - Busy Bags - Sensory - Practical Life - Early Learning - Art & Crafts - Seasonal & Holiday {1}

A Note About Safety:

The activities in this book are intended to be done under adult supervision. Appropriate and reasonable caution is required at all times. Beware when using all materials and tools suggested in this book, including but not limited to scissors, hot glue or objects that could pose a choking hazard. Observe safety and caution at all times. The authors of this book disclaim all liability for any damage, mishap or injury that may occur from engaging in activities in this book.

Copyright:

Text and photographs copyright by their respective authors.

All rights reserved. No part of this book may be reproduced in any form or by any means, electronic or mechanical, including photocopying, recording, or by any information storage and retrieval system, without permission in writing from the publisher and authors.

First Edition | 2016

Disclaimer:

The authors of this book are not affiliated with any of the products used or displayed for fine motor skill crafts, activities and ideas.

LEGO®is a trademark of the LEGO Group of companies which does not sponsor, authorize or endorse this book.

Reviews for 99 Fine Motor Ideas

- As a pediatric occupational therapist, I'm always looking for new fine motor ideas for my kids at work. This book is FULL of simple, quick-on-the-draw fine motor activities for all ages and ability levels. I'll be keeping this resource handy in my therapy room as I plan my treatment sessions each week! - theinspiredtreehouse

- This book is both beautiful and practical! I love the variety of play ideas for toddlers and preschoolers, and I can't wait to get started with my three-year-old. These are simple, inexpensive, and engaging ideas. - Annaon

- As a occupational therapist who works with children from 0 -3, I think this is a great resource for therapists, parents and educators! The activities are fun, colorful and address the fine motor skills little ones need to develop! The games are so easy to make and frequently use things available in the home, and the pictures and directions are easy to follow. - Amanda F

- This book is jam packed with amazing fine motor ideas! It's geared towards toddlers/preschoolers, but most of the ideas can be modified for the K-2 level as well!! As a teacher, I can't wait to try some of these in my classroom to help differentiate some of my learning. As a mother-to-be, I can't wait to start collecting a bunch of the materials (which are usually found in your home) so I can start developing my baby girl's fine motor skills early! The book also has fun facts about each author (which is one of my favorite parts). The materials and what you will need are all written in as well! The pictures and colors are very clean and vibrant, so I can see toddlers being able to go through with a parent and choose an activity to do! - Furnell T

- 99 Fine Motor Ideas is the perfect thing to stock a family's or preschool's bookshelf. It is an education boredom buster! I love watching my three-year-old daughter grab it from the shelf, open and peruse through the pages, investigating the possibilities. The play ideas are simple and affordable, based on many things commonly found around the home. A single page from this book can initiate a new perspective on fine motor play and encourage children to follow directions and keep them peacefully playing for a while. The games and crafts provoke insightful questioning and testing of the local environment, constructively teaching kids to manipulate their surroundings. As a mom, this book inspires me to look at our play things in a new light and I feel happy to provide simple yet stimulating homemade play for my daughter. 99 Fine Motor Ideas is an indispensable resource for creative at home play. - Jessica H

- This is the most complete book of fun and age appropriate ideas. Worth every cent and so much easier than looking things up online all of the time. Instructions are complete as well as illustrations. - Amazon Fan

- 99 Fine Motor Ideas is a great resource for parents, preschools and homeschoolers that I highly recommend. We have used many of the ideas in our program and adapted others to come up with our own new creations! Each activity comes with a supplies list of things you will probably already have on hand, and an easy to follow "How to", plus great pictures! These activities are "tried and true" and will bring hours of learning and FUN! Best of all we can do them in our classroom and then refer parents to the book, so they can continue and extend the learning at home." Carol Anne F

- I love this book!!! I use it both as a professional working in early intervention and as the parent of a young child! The ideas are great and have really helped me provide fun activities to practice fine motor skills, even with kids that can be difficult to engage and don't want to "work." The activities are well thought out and nicely presented, making it easy for me to replicate them. They're always a big hit, both at home and at work! - Crystal C., Early Intervention Developmental Specialist

Toys - Busy Bags - Sensory - Practical Life - Early Learning - Art & Crafts - Seasonal & Holiday

About the Authors

Nicolette Roux - Powerful Mothering

Nicolette is a stay-at-home mom to four little ones ages six years and under. She loves to share her simple and easy crafts & activities, printables, and learning ideas for babies, toddlers, and preschoolers!

Visit Nicolette's Blog at: www.powerfulmothering.com

Laura Marschel - Lalymom

Laura is mom to two sweet redheads who fuel all the fun over at Lalymom.com. She shares cool kids crafts, fun activities, free printables and parenting tips too! It's basically all about having fun!

Visit Laura's Blog at: www.lalymom.com

Blayne Burke - House of Burke

A WAHM mom and blogger at House of Burke, Blayne has two sons: a spirited ginger haired preschooler and an adventurous toddler. Her blog and books focus on crafts and activities for infants-preschoolers. She spends her days homeschooling her two boys, crafting, and creating. Together as a family, they love exploring and learning about the world around them!

Visit Blayne's Blog at: www.houseofburkeblog.com

Georgina Bomer - Craftulate

Craftulate features art, craft, and activities for young children. Georgina enjoys working her son's interests into their daily activities to help him learn and develop. She is the author of Art, Craft & Cooking with Toddlers and 50 Animal Crafts for Little Kids.

Visit Georgina's Blog at: www.craftulate.com

Photo credit: Karen Reichley

Devany LeDrew - Still Playing School

Devany LeDrew from Still Playing School is a former kindergarten teacher turned write-at-home-mom of six year old E, baby girl Violet (who only lived 2.5 days in 2011), and three year old D. She creates play based learning invitations for E & D as she combines her background in Early Childhood Education and Educational Psychology with her passion for homeschooling. She also writes about grief, how they remember Violet, and how meeting and losing her has changed them all forever.

Visit Devany's Blog at: www.stillplayingschool.com

Sarah McClelland - Little Bins For Little Hands

Sarah is a stay-at-home mom of one busy boy. She enjoys incorporating important fine motor skills practice into a variety of hands-on learning activities that her son enjoys. Sarah's blog focuses on science, sensory, and STEM activities for learning and play. Together she and her son explore the world through creative activities and experiments.

Visit Sarah's Blog at: www.littlebinsforlittlehands.com

Kristina Couturier - School Time Snippets

Kristina is a homeschooling mother of four. With children of various ages from infant to eight years old, Kristina shares a variety of educational and play activities for babies, toddlers, preschoolers, and early elementary aged children on her blog, School Time Snippets.

Visit Kristina's Blog at: www.schooltimesnippets.com

Dyan Robson - And Next Comes L

Dyan is the Canadian mom and part time piano teacher behind the blog And Next Comes L. She is married to her high school sweetheart and has two sons. Her blog focuses on autism, hyperlexia, hypernumeracy, and sensory resources.

Visit Dyan's Blog at: www.andnextcomesL.com

Emma Craig - Our Whimsical Days

Emma is a stay-at-home mom to a six year old daughter. She loves to share fun and interactive learning activities and simple play ideas through her blog, Our Whimsical Days.

Visit Emma's Blog at: www.ourwhimsicaldays.com

Samantha Soper-Caetano - Stir the Wonder

Samantha is a stay-at-home mom to an active preschooler. She loves thinking of creative ways to engage her son in hands-on learning, including fine motor activities, sensory play, nature exploration, science experiments, and book-inspired ideas!

Visit Samantha's Blog at: www.stirthewonder.com

Toys - Busy Bags - Sensory - Practical Life - Early Learning - Art & Crafts - Seasonal & Holiday

Table of Contents

1. Toys (p8-25)

Packing Peanuts and Toothpicks Building Game 10
Foam Animals Building Set 11
Fix-It Box 12
Feeding the Lion 13
Nest Toy 14
DIY Bull's Eye Game 15
Personalized Photo Finger Puppets 16
Blocks 17
PVC Pipe Building Kit 18
Play Dough Small World 19
Marble Tube Play 20
Shrinky Dinks Lacing Shapes 21
Twisty Cups 22
Cardboard Stackers 23
Musical Shakers 24
Painting Peg People 25

3. Sensory (p42-57)

Play Dough Balloons 44
Citrus Scented Salt Tray 45
LEGO® Sensory Soup 46
Pre-Writing Squish Bag 47
Shape Sorting Sensory Play 48
Life-Size Pom Pom Pit 49
Moon Dust Writing Tray 50
Sensory Sound Blocks 51
Search and Find Slime 52
Color Sorting on the Light Table 53
Taste-Safe Kinetic Sand Play 54
Play Dough Surprise 55
Fine Motor Beach Activities 56
Treasure Hunting 57

2. Busy Bags (p26-41)

Paperclip Color Match 28
Pool Noodles & Rubber Bands Busy Bag 29
Space Alien Busy Bag 30
Velcro and Foam Chain 31
Paper Punching 32
Paper Clip Chain 33
Aluminum Foil Roll 34
Button Sorting 35
Lacing Beads 36
Building with Straws and Play Dough 37
Threading Washers and Nuts 38
Rainbow Bubble Wrap Busy Bag 39
Counting Sticks 40
Body Part Matching Game 41

4. Practical Life (p58-71)

Food and Snack Preparation 60
Washing Clothes 61
Busy Tray 62
Towel Folding Activity 63
Window Washing Tray 64
Bike Washing 65
Gift Wrapping Invitation to Play 66
Open and Close Treasure Basket 67
Silly Sammy Scissors Practice 68
Pet Care 69
Making Lemonade 70
Time to Brush! 71

5. Early Learning (p72-89)

Color Size Match Activity 74
Peeling Tape Letters Pre-Writing Activity 75
Button Music Theory Art 76
Name Recognition with Clothespegs 77
ABC Fish Matching 78
Name Bracelet 79
Counting Ants Sensory Game 80
Count and Stack Game 81
Crumpled Paper ABC Basketball 82
Kitchen Science Experiment 83
Rainbow Ball 84
Patterning Activity 85
Jar Lid Busy Box 86
Play Dough Pinch & Roll Counting Game 87
Object Trace 88
Smashing ABC Moon Rocks 89

7. Seasonal Holidays (p106-121)

Cake Decorating Craft 108
Groundhog Finger Puppet 109
Valentine's Day Loom Band Hearts 110
Painting Rainbows with Combs 111
Easter Garland 112
Easter Egg Match 113
Apple Color Sorting Tray 114
Pumpkin Patch 115
Spooky Spider Web 116
Clothespin Feathers Turkey 117
Candy Cane Garland 118
Gumdrop Structures 119
Paper Plate Christmas Wreath 120
Baked Cotton Ball Snowman 121

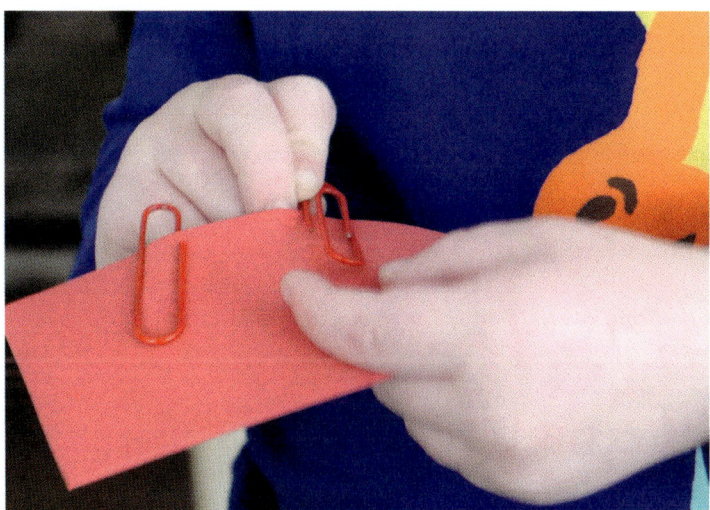

6. Art & Crafts (p90-105)

Owl Collage 92
Easy Cut Punch Paste Crafting 93
Powdered Chalk Art 94
Yarn Wrapped Music Notes 95
Watercolor Drop Painted Bunting 96
Beaded Wind Chime 97
Pom Pom Rainbow 98
Clay Pinch Pots 99
Symmetrical Butterfly Straw Painting 100
Yarn Mobiles 101
Spaghetti Sun 102
Cotton Swab Steam Train Art 103
Stained Glass Art 104
Seashell Ladybugs 105

Author Links (p123)

Index (p125-127)

Printables (p128-137)

Toys - Busy Bags - Sensory - Practical Life - Early Learning - Art & Crafts - Seasonal & Holiday

Toys

Packing Peanuts and Toothpicks Building Game by Georgina, Craftulate

Foam Animals Building Set by Dyan, And Next Comes L

Fix-It Box by Emma, Our Whimsical Days

Feeding the Lion by Blayne, House of Burke

Nest Toy by Blayne, House of Burke

DIY Bull's Eye Game by Sarah, Little Bins For Little Hands

Personalized Photo Finger Puppets by Devany, Still Playing School

Blocks by Nicolette, Powerful Mothering

PVC Pipe Building Kit by Sarah, Little Bins For Little Hands

Play Dough Small World by Kristina, School Time Snippets

Marble Tube Play by Emma, Our Whimsical Days

Shrinky Dinks Lacing Shapes by Laura, Lalymom

Twisty Cups by Laura, Lalymom

Cardboard Stackers by Nicolette, Powerful Mothering

Musical Shakers by Nicolette, Powerful Mothering

Painting Peg People by Blayne, House of Burke

Packing Peanuts and Toothpicks Building Game

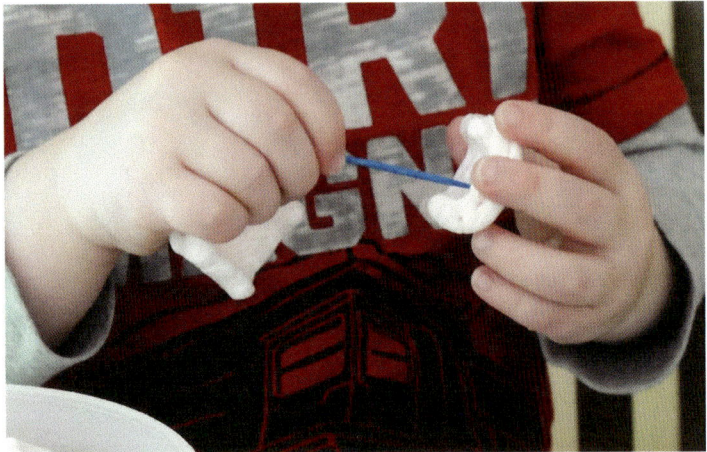

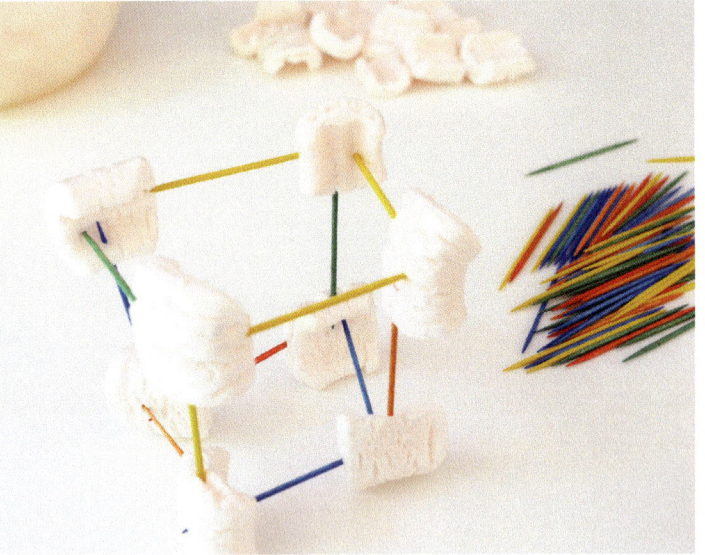

How to

No preparation is required here. Just provide your child with the materials and let them get building! Show them how to carefully insert a toothpick into one of the packing peanuts. Make sure they know to do go slowly so that they don't accidentally push the toothpick into their hand!

Then show them how to add another peanut to the opposite end of the toothpick. If they add two more, then they can make a square which forms a great base for building!

This game needs creativity, patience, and concentration, but most importantly, it really works on fine motor skills – the pincer grasp on the toothpick and the hand-eye coordination required for inserting it into the peanut.

Start with geometric 3D shapes like cubes, cuboids, and pyramids (the pyramids can have either a triangular or square base). Once your child has mastered the technique, they will probably just want to build higher and higher!

by **Georgina Bomer**
Craftulate
Making. Learning. Fun.
www.craftulate.com

Materials / Supplies

- Styrofoam packing peanuts
- Wooden toothpicks (cocktail sticks)

Notes / Tips

Variation: This game would be a great activity for a classroom to work together and build a huge structure!

Foam Animals Building Set

by **Dyan Robson**
And Next Comes L
Hyperlexia + Autism + Other Tales of Learning
www.andnextcomesL.com

Materials / Supplies

- Craft foam sheets
- Scissors
- Clothespins
- Permanent markers

How to

This foam animal building kit makes a great mix and match toy set for kids, but it also works great as a busy bag for on the go. Kids will enjoy matching the limbs to the correct body or mixing them up to create fun new creatures like zebra-pigs! And when the clothespins are attached to the animal's body, the animal can stand on its clothespin legs.

To make these adorable fine motor animals, cut out an animal body shape from a piece of craft foam. Decorate the craft foam with details like stripes, spots, eyes, etc. using the permanent markers. Draw matching details on the clothespins for the animal's tail and legs. I made all of these animals double sided so that the zebra's stripes, for example, would show on both the front and back of the body and legs. Then they're ready for playtime! Kids can either match the legs to the correct body or mix and match them.

Notes / Tips

Try making an elephant and use a clothespin for the elephant's trunk.

Fix-It Box

by **Emma Craig**
Our Whimsical Days
Memories in the making
www.ourwhimsicaldays.com

Materials / Supplies

- Child's tool set
- Cardboard box
- Rubber band (optional)

How to

After my daughter got a toolbox for her third birthday, she went around the house asking if there was anything she could "fix." She would bang, saw, and measure on the chairs, the sofa, and pretty much anything else. But she wanted something more real. Enter...the fix-it box.

This fix-it box is ridiculously simple and we have gone through many over the years. All it takes is a fairly sturdy cardboard box. The perfect box would be a durable one with a lid, which would allow you to store the tools inside! Poke random holes in the top for the "nails." Kids can hammer them or use the screwdriver to push them in. Adding a rubber band can make a fun twang sound when it is sawed or even just plucked.

This simple idea can keep little ones busy for so long, and little do they realize, how much fine motor practice they are getting at the same time.

Notes / Tips

To really make it their own, suggest your child paint or color the fix-it box first!

Feeding the Lion

by **Blayne Burke**
House of Burke
Learning and exploring together as a family!
www.houseofburkeblog.com

Materials / Supplies

- Shoebox (cover removed)
- Printed picture of lion
- Tape
- Straws
- Small bag clip or clothespin

How to

This ferocious fine motor toy will have your little one engaged in a roaring good time! To make your lion, you will need a small, coverless box. A shoebox works great or a clementine crate like we used here. Find a picture of a lion and print it out. Make sure it is large enough to cover the entire piece of paper. Attach it to the box by taping the corners. Then, punch a hole in the center of the lion's mouth using a straw.

Then you are ready to set up your invitation to play. Gather a bunch of straws and place them in front of the box. Set a small bag clip up next to the straws. Encourage your little one to feed the lion by taking the bag clip and using it to pick up one of the straws. Both the act of pinching the clip and placing it in the small hole of the mouth works both fine motor skills and spatial reasoning skills.

After they have fed the lion several times, you can add in some more learning components. Ask them to feed the lion a certain amount of straws or a certain color. You could even combine the two tasks for some joint number and color learning! You can also pretend that the straws are different food items that you are feeding to the lion. When your lion is "full," gently untape the bottom and dump them out. You can use your lion again and again for some wild fine motor play!

This activity would be great to pair with a zoo trip! Have your little one observe what their favorite animal is eating, then come home and set this up!

Notes / Tips

If your little one does not love lions, switch it up! You can print out virtually any animal or dinosaur instead.

Nest Toy

by **Blayne Burke**
House of Burke
Learning and exploring together as a family!
www.houseofburkeblog.com

How to

My favorite toys for my kids are ones that are multi-faceted. Homemade toys are even better! They cost little to nothing to make and can be created with simple materials found around your home. This nest toy encourages the use of fine motor skills, imaginative play, and hand-eye coordination.

To create your homemade nest, take a small round basket and cover the top with plastic wrap. Make sure to pull the plastic wrap as tightly as possible so that the opening you cut is easily accessible to your little one. Cut a slit in the center, about 4 inches, using your scissors. Set out a pile of feathers and a pair of plastic tweezers.

Encourage your little one to help the birds build a cozy nest! Invite them to use the tweezers to pick up each feather and place them in the opening. As they put them in and begin to cover the bottom of the basket, it will begin to look like a cozy spot for their bird friends. As they give their fine motor skills a workout, involve them in a conversation about birds and their homes. Discuss such topics as where nests are located, what kind of birds may live in them, and how real birds build their nests.

When they have placed all of their feathers in the basket, remove the plastic wrap and let them place their bird toys inside. Use this time to encourage them to engage in pretend play with the new habitat and their birds.

Materials / Supplies

- Small basket
- Plastic wrap
- Scissors
- Feathers
- Plastic tweezers
- Pretend bird(s)

Notes / Tips

Incorporate color and number learning by asking them to place a specific color feather in their nest or a certain amount of feathers. Combine the two for the ultimate learning experience!

DIY Bull's Eye Game

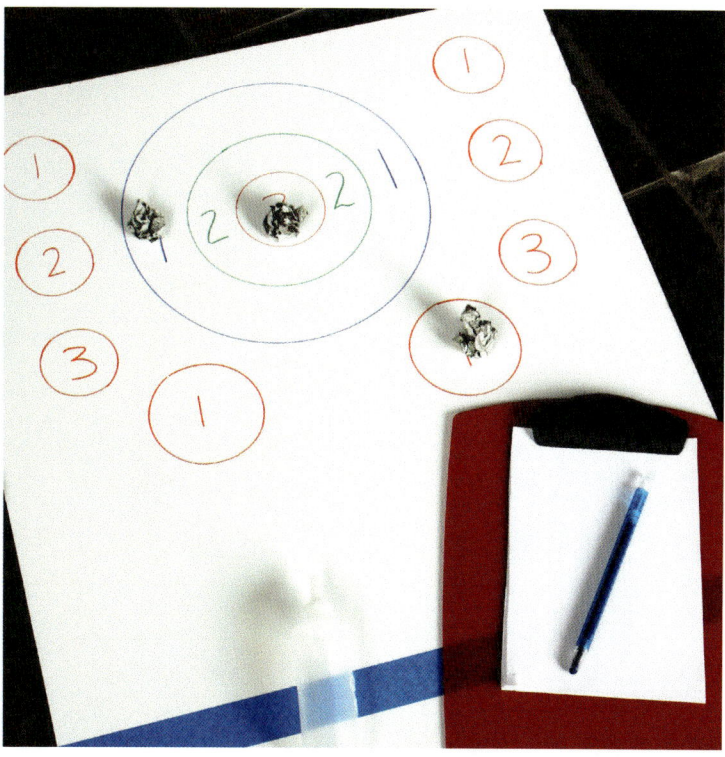

by **Sarah McClelland**
Little Bins For Little Hands
A Sensory Filled Life
www.littlebinsforlittlehands.com

Materials / Supplies

- Large piece of foam board or poster board
- Painters tape or similar
- Small squeeze bottle
- Markers for drawing circles and writing in numbers
- Circular items to trace (or try it freehand!)
- Crumpled newspaper or tissue paper
- Optional: pad of paper and pen to keep track of score

Notes / Tips

Change the rules to fit the needs of your kids! We added a second chance rule if the ball didn't even make it to the bull's eye. You could also add a scoring option by writing numbers or making simple tally marks.

How to

This DIY, quick, and easy table game is perfect for improving fine motor skills, practicing counting and number recognition, and encouraging visual processing skills. Squeezing is a simple fine motor activity that will increase hand strength.

To set up your game, draw a bull's eye at the top of a foam board. Tracing different sized bowls from the pantry is an easy way to make the bull's eye. For our version, we started with a traditional bull's eye style board, but then decided to add mini circles on the sides for more fun and play. Use any colors you like and practice color recognition too. Next, add a strip of painter's tape down by the bottom of the board. This shows each player where to place his or her hands! We also added numbers to our circles to turn it into a family math game.

Grab some newspaper or tissue paper and a small squeeze bottle to get the game started. Crumple the tissue paper or newspaper into small balls. Test the size of your paper balls. The first ones we made were a little too big and did not move as far with our small squeeze bottle. Once you have a good size, get set to test your fine motor skills!

Each player receives the same amount of balls. We used three per person, so there are three chances to score. Place thumbs on top of the bottle with the backs of fingers firmly on the blue tape. The thumbs will do the squeezing action. Make sure you have the squeeze bottle pointing into the paper ball. Give a quick squeeze and see where your paper ball lands. Did you get a bull's eye?

Personalized Photo Finger Puppets

by **Devany LeDrew**
Still Playing School
Playing, learning, remembering
www.stillplayingschool.com

Materials / Supplies

- Craft foam
- Tape
- Stapler
- Hole punch
- Printed photos of your kids
- Scissors

How to

Use your family's photos to create personalized finger puppets for hours of fine motor fun!

Cut the puppet bodies and clothing from craft foam. Tape the pieces together reinforcing with staples as needed. Use a hole punch to make increasingly larger circles on the legs until your kids' fingers can fit through the holes. You could also use a larger hole punch instead.

Take a photo of your child looking directly at the camera. Print on regular paper or cardstock - or photo paper for the most durability. Cut out the face and attach it to your puppet! Enjoy storytelling scenarios with your personalized puppets!

Notes / Tips

Children can decorate their own outfits with markers, stickers, and washi tape!

Blocks

by **Nicolette Roux**
Powerful Mothering
Learning one step at a time
www.PowerfulMothering.com

Materials / Supplies

- Wooden blocks
- Food dye
- Vinegar
- Velcro dots
- Plastic cutting knife

How to

There are so many things that kids can do with blocks! Did you know that you can dye your own wooden blocks? It is easy to do! To stain the wooden blocks, place plain wooden blocks in some food dye mixed with a bit of vinegar (approximately one tablespoon of vinegar to three drops of dye). Once they are dry, you can hand them over to the kids!

Stack the blocks in a tower and see how high they can go. If you have made multiple colors, then you can also use the blocks as a color sorting exercise.

For the cutting game, use Velcro dots to join the blocks together. Encourage your child to cut them apart using the plastic knife.

Notes / Tips

If you made rainbow color blocks, then your child could even sort to the rainbow!

PVC Pipe Building Kit

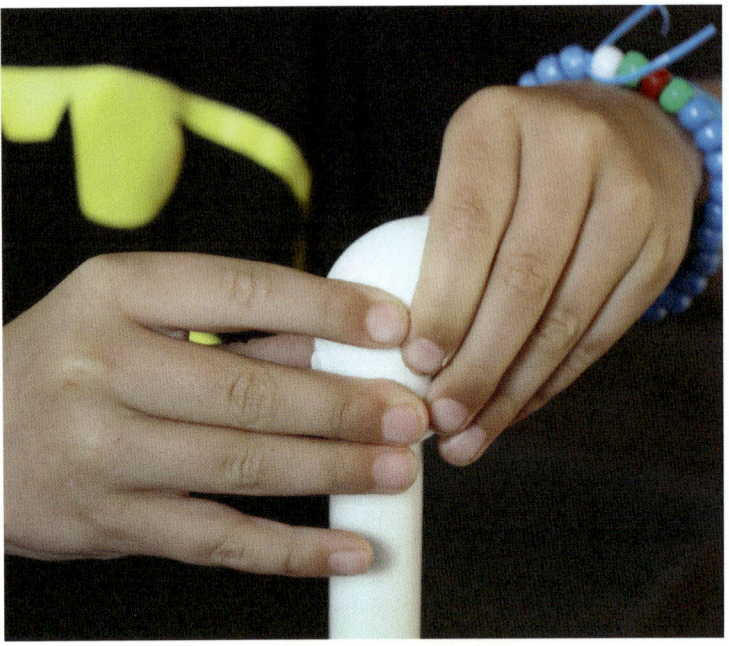

Materials / Supplies

- PVC plastic pipes - found in the plumbing departments of hardware stores
- PVC pipe fittings - various angles
- Small saw
- Sandpaper
- Container

by **Sarah McClelland**
Little Bins For Little Hands
A Sensory Filled Life
www.littlebinsforlittlehands.com

How to

I made a simple fine motor building kit out of PVC plastic pipes and pipe fittings from our local hardware store. I chose the smallest plastic pipes available. Your store may cut the plastic pipe for you. If not, you can use a small saw to cut the pipe into the sizes that you need. Make sure to use sandpaper to smooth the edges when finished.

I cut various size pieces from two inches to twelve inches long. I also bought a few bags of various pipe fittings in different angles to create a variety of play ideas.

This PVC plastic pipe building toy kit is great for hand strength and hand-eye coordination. It is simple enough for a young child to use, but great for an older child as well. Young kids will simply enjoy connecting the pipes while older kids can build cool structures! The longer the pipes, the more gross motor play is involved too!

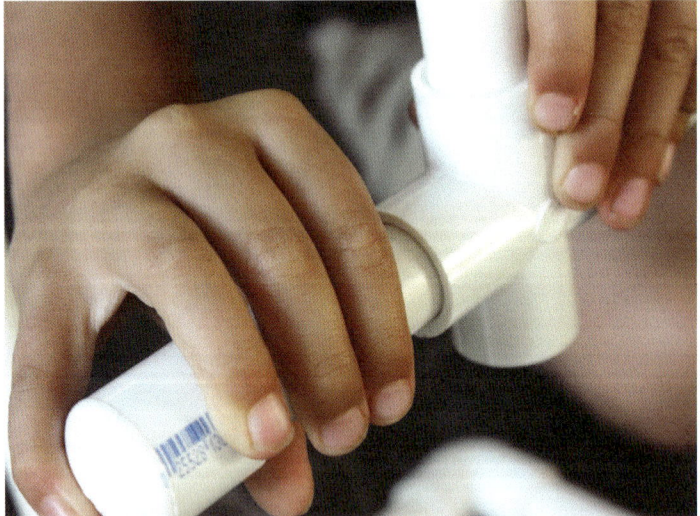

Notes / Tips

My son added his super hero characters to the structures. We even created a house and added cardboard floors! We have made hearts and a working pulley by adding rope and a cup. Kids can color the plastic pipes with permanent markers to make fun colors and designs!

Play Dough Small World

by **Kristina Couturier**
School Time Snippets
Learn and play today
www.schooltimesnippets.com

Materials / Supplies

- Green play dough
- Blue play dough
- Glass gems
- Fake flowers
- Small plastic fairies
- Scissors

Notes / Tips

If your kids are not into fairies, try dinosaurs instead! Or make an ocean small world with glass gems and play dough! Take your child's interest, add in a few extra manipulatives, some play dough, and you have your own small world!

How to

This play dough small world is to make a Fairy Garden Small World, but is adaptable to many other themes. Creating a small world using play dough and small manipulatives is great for fine motor skills.

To make this simple Fairy Garden Small World, gather all the materials and begin creating! Manipulate the play dough to make your scene. Pinch, roll, mold the green play dough for the "land" and blue play dough for the water.

Have your child create a whimsical garden by cutting down the stems of the plastic flowers and inserting the flowers into the play dough. Add in glass gems to create a fairy path.

Now that your small world is set up, add your fairies and let the pretend play begin!

Marble Tube Play

How to

This activity is very simple, but my five year old was at it for a good 45 minutes and asked for it again the next day!

We used a clear plastic tube from a home improvement store, but there are colorful plastic tubes at most dollar stores that would work just as well.

Let your child explore and see where they go with it. It is an open-ended activity - no right or wrong way to do it. Picking up the marbles and putting them in the tube is great fine motor practice. My daughter loved trying to get the marbles to "jump" into a box she put out (unknowingly adding a little science into the mix!). Rolling the marbles back and forth inside the tube was also popular.

by **Emma Craig**
Our Whimsical Days
Memories in the making
www.ourwhimsicaldays.com

Materials / Supplies

- Plastic tubing
- Marbles

Notes / Tips

For an extra fine motor challenge, try using water beads instead of marbles!

Shrinky Dinks Lacing Shapes

by **Laura Marschel**
Lalymom
Home with two, creativity will brew
www.Lalymom.com

Materials / Supplies

- Scissors
- 1-3 Shrinky Dinks sheets or other brand shrink film
- 3/8 inch or ½ inch hole punch
- Permanent markers
- Laces
- Oven
- Parchment paper
- Sheet pan
- Wire baking rack (recommended, optional)

Notes / Tips

Curling and lifting up are totally normal when shrinking shrinky dinks. The parchment and wire rack help prevent it from curling so much that it sticks to itself. If you do not use the wire rack and parchment, then keep an eye on the pieces and only open the oven if a piece looks like they are curling enough to stick to itself, then use a heat proof tool like a spatula to pry it apart. With time, it will flatten back out in the oven.

How to

Cut out your desired shapes from your shrink film. Make your shapes as large as the sheets allow, keeping in mind that they will shrink by at least half. Round the corners if you want to avoid sharp corners.

Using your 3/8 inch or ½ inch paper punch, punch holes around the edge, about 1.5 to 2 inches apart. (Tip: if you turn your punch upside down you can see exactly where you will be punching.)

Use the markers to trace the outline of your shapes in whatever decorative way you like.

Preheat your oven to 325F degrees and turn on the vent fan. Line your sheet pan with a large piece of parchment paper folded in half. Place your pieces in between the parchment paper so that they are at least an inch apart. Work in batches if they do not all fit. Place the wire baking rack upside down over the parchment paper. There should be a little space between your pieces and the wire rack.

Place in the oven and set a timer for ten minutes. When they have stopped shrinking remove the pan, slide the parchment onto a heat safe counter and allow to cool. Now they are ready for lacing!

Twisty Cups

Materials / Supplies

- 2 clear plastic cups, the bigger the better
- Permanent Markers and/or stickers

by **Laura Marschel**
Lalymom
Home with two, creativity will brew
www.Lalymom.com

How to

Use your markers or stickers to create a maze or design on one cup, then add one sticker or drawing to the other cup. Be sure to pay attention to where the second cup lines up with the first cup when you place your sticker or drawing on it.

When your designs are complete be sure to allow time for the ink to dry. Then nest the two cups together and show your child how to twist them to complete the maze or puzzle.

Variations:

Car Track: Draw a start line at the bottom of your first cup, then draw a race track winding up and around the cup. Draw a finish line at the end of the track, near the rim. Draw a truck near the bottom of the second cup.

Number Munch: Place number stickers on the first cup in a winding or random pattern. Draw a PacMan or other munching character near the bottom of the second cup. Show your child how to make him munch the numbers in order.

Color Mixing: Draw single circles of primary colors on each cup. Show your child how they can be twisted and stacked to mix the colors.

Notes / Tips

I could think of a million themes for these cup twist games! Holidays, cartoons- any theme that your child is interested in!

Cardboard Stackers

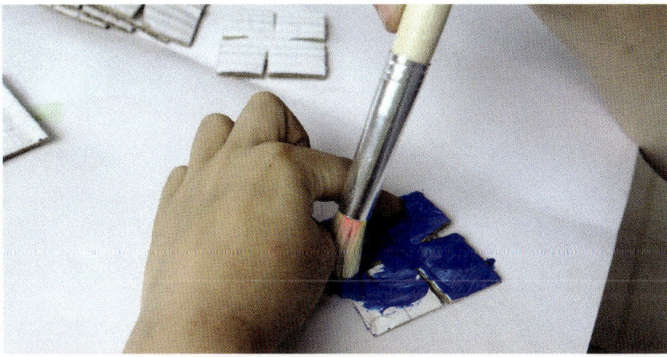

by **Nicolette Roux**
Powerful Mothering
Learning one step at a time
www.PowerfulMothering.com

Materials / Supplies

- Cardboard
- Scissors
- Paint
- Newspaper

How to

Cut out squares or rectangles of cardboard in the same size. The easiest way to do so is by making a grid on the cardboard before cutting.

Once you have all of the shapes, make the slits by cutting twice relatively close to each other (see image for example). I cut half of my shapes like this and left the other half uncut.

Lay the cardboard stackers on some newspaper and paint the top and bottom and then let it dry.

Once the cardboard stackers are dry, have fun building all sorts of towers and structures with them!

Notes / Tips

My kids loved the challenge of who can get the highest tower without it falling over! It is a great lesson in building a foundation.

Musical Shakers

by **Nicolette Roux**
Powerful Mothering
Learning one step at a time
www.PowerfulMothering.com

Materials / Supplies

- Clear plastic bottles
- Feathers
- Buttons
- Beads
- Pom poms
- Hot glue (optional)

How to

These homemade musical shakers are great to make for young children who may still mouth small objects.

To make the shakers, first sort the items for each bottle. We added feathers and buttons to one bottle, pom poms and beads to another, and the third bottle just had beads in it. Then encourage your children to make the musical shaker bottles by themselves. Hot glue the lids closed if you prefer.

Rolling the bottles around is a great visual experience for the kids; shaking them can result in spontaneous dance, and because each bottle has different things in them, you can play the loud / loudest game with them.

Notes / Tips

If you have multiple aged children, the older children could make a special bottle for the younger child.

Painting Peg People

by **Blayne Burke**
House of Burke
Learning and exploring together as a family!
www.houseofburkeblog.com

Materials / Supplies

- Wooden peg dolls
- Acrylic paints
- Paint brushes in varying sizes
- Varnish spray

Notes / Tips

If your little one has a favorite character, help them design their very own peg version! You can look at pictures for reference and talk to them about what they need to use to make a look-a-like peg.

How to

Peg dolls are such a fun way to let your creativity shine. My kids both love their collection of peg people, and letting them create their own allows them to let their imaginations run wild.

To start making your peg dolls, you need to pick up a pack of unfinished wooden dolls. They come in all shapes and sizes, so choose whichever one seems the most appropriate for your child. Set out your wooden pegs and a variety of paints and brushes. Make sure your brushes are small and thin enough that your little one can have control over the surface area they are painting.

Encourage your child to paint their peg people to the best of their capabilities. Using the differently sized paintbrushes will work their fine motor skills, while painting the clothing will encourage hand-eye coordination. Younger toddlers will most likely paint without any sense of clothing, but take the chance to engage them in a discussion about clothing. Preschoolers and older children may enjoy choosing two colors and painting pants and a shirt. If they are able to, they can add details when they dry or you can! Painting peg people is just as fun for adults!

When their peg people are finished, spray with a non-toxic varnish spray. Our peg people have been known to get chewed on every once in awhile, so you want to make sure that your little one is staying safe!

Busy Bags

Paperclip Color Match by Georgina, Craftulate

Pool Noodles & Rubber Bands Busy Bag by Dyan, And Next Comes L

Space Alien Busy Bag by Samantha, Stir the Wonder

Velcro and Foam Chain by Kristina, School Time Snippets

Paper Punching by Kristina, School Time Snippets

Paper Clip Chain by Emma, Our Whimsical Days

Aluminum Foil Roll by Blayne, House of Burke

Button Sorting by Nicolette, Powerful Mothering

Lacing Beads by Devany, Still Playing School

Building with Straws and Play Dough by Sarah, Little Bins for Little Hands

Threading Washers and Nuts by Sarah, Little Bins for Little Hands

Rainbow Bubble Wrap Busy Bag by Laura, Lalymom

Counting Sticks by Nicolette, Powerful Mothering

Body Part Matching Game by Blayne, House of Burke

Paperclip Color Match

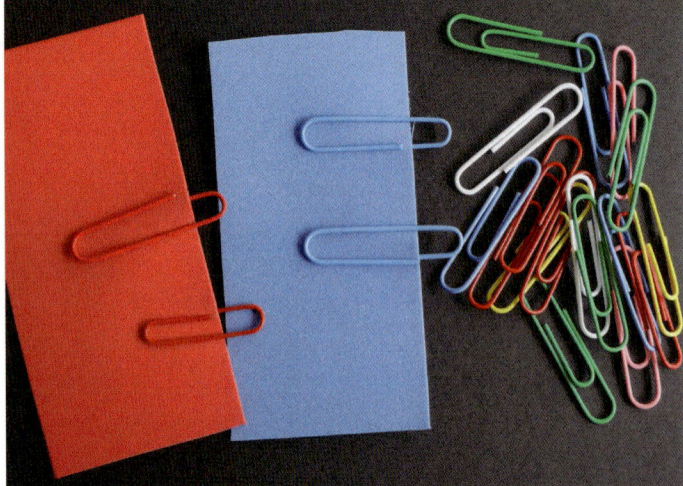

How to

The only preparation needed for this activity is to collect the materials and match up the colors of your craft foam to the paperclips that you have. I prefer to use craft foam as it is a bit more resilient than colored cardstock. Cardstock can easily get damaged after little hands have tried to repeatedly fasten on the paperclips.

Invite your child to match up the paperclip to the correct color craft foam. If they are unfamiliar with manipulating paperclips, then you may need to demonstrate how to attach them. It will take lots of concentration, hand-eye coordination, and finger strength to achieve this goal!

Once they have mastered fastening the paperclips to the craft foam, you could suggest that they try and fasten the paperclips to each other, forming long chains of paperclips of the same color attached to the correct piece of craft foam.

by **Georgina Bomer**
Craftulate
Making. Learning. Fun.
www.craftulate.com

Materials / Supplies

- Colored paperclips
- Craft foam sheets or colored cardstock
- Bag or container

Notes / Tips

Extend the activity further by working in some counting practice. Write a number on each piece of craft foam then ask your child to attach the correct number of paperclips.

{28} 100 Fine Motor Ideas

Pool Noodles & Rubber Bands Busy Bag

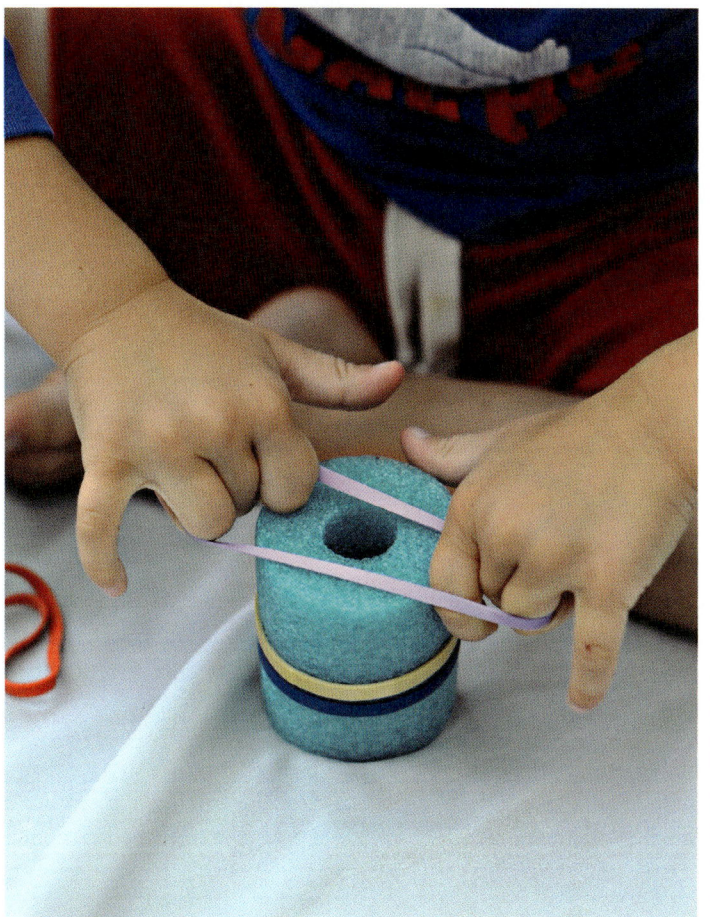

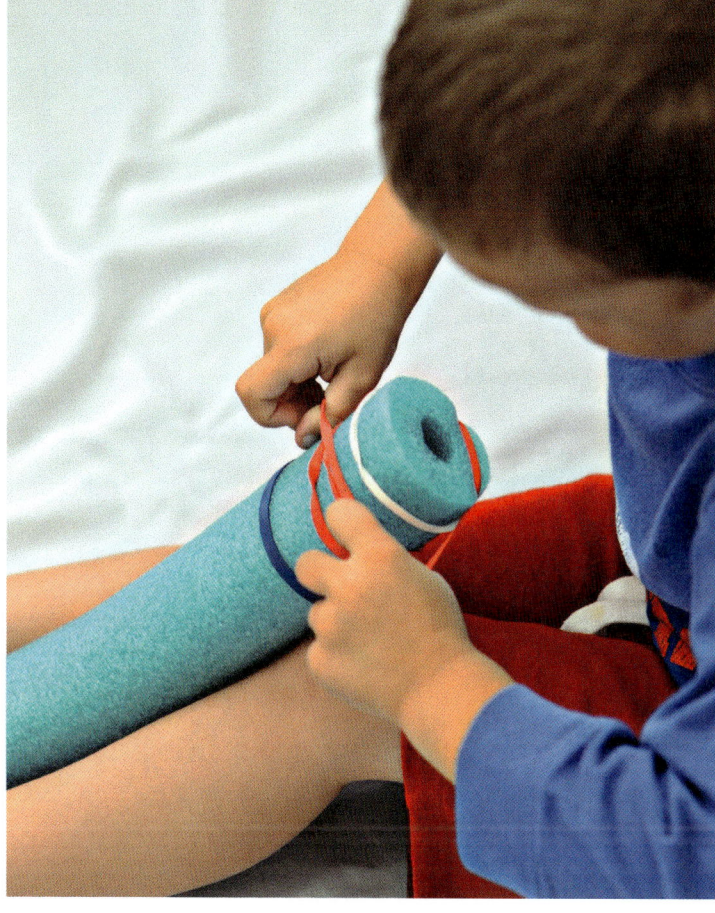

by **Dyan Robson**
And Next Comes L
Hyperlexia + Autism + Other Tales of Learning
www.andnextcomesL.com

Materials / Supplies

- Pool noodles
- Large knife or utility knife to cut the pool noodles
- Rubber bands

Notes / Tips

Have no pool noodles kicking around? Try this activity using canned goods instead.

How to

This busy bag is ridiculously simple, but my kids love it!

Simply cut a pool noodle into various lengths and set out some rubber bands. The object of this activity is to stretch the rubber bands around the pool noodle. Stretching the rubber bands helps to strengthen little hands.

As my kids experimented with the different lengths of pool noodles, they found that the smaller pieces of pool noodles were more challenging to get the rubber bands onto, simply because they were not able to hold onto the pool noodle as easily. My three year old preferred the longer pool noodles because he could hold it between his knees while adding rubber bands to it.

Space Alien Busy Bag

How to

If your kids enjoy playing with Mr. Potato Head, then they will love this simple fine motor activity! Plus, it is easily stored in a plastic zip bag making it an ideal busy bag for appointments, restaurants, or traveling.

Cut out a round shape using the sticker backed craft foam. This foam works best because it is a little bit stiffer and will not get weighed down by the clips as easily. You could also use cardboard.

Draw a simple mouth on the alien head using permanent marker and place a self-adhesive velcro dot in the center.

Draw different space alien parts on colorful craft foam. Some ideas to include are arms, sock-like legs, alien ears, some antenna, and different eyes.

Cut out all the parts and use a hot glue gun to attach googly eyes and the clothespins.

Optional: Use glitter glue or colorful permanent markers to add details to the space alien parts. Some fun details to include are eyebrows, eyelashes, teeth, fingernails, and sock details.

by **Samantha Soper-Caetano**
Stir the Wonder
Inspiring Learning
www.stirthewonder.com

Materials / Supplies

- 1 sheet of sticky-back craft foam
- Regular craft foam in a variety of colors
- Clothespins
- Googly eyes
- Hot glue gun
- Permanent marker
- Velcro dots
- Glitter glue (optional)
- Colorful permanent markers (optional)

Notes / Tips

The more creative your space alien parts, the more fun your kids will have practicing their fine motor skills and hand-eye coordination! A fun variation of this activity would be to create silly monsters instead.

Velcro and Foam Chain

by **Kristina Couturier**
School Time Snippets
Learn and play today
www.schooltimesnippets.com

Materials / Supplies

- Craft foam sheets
- Velcro dots
- Scissors

How to

This Velcro and foam chain busy bag is quite easy to put together.

With several sheets of craft foam, cut each piece into 1-2 inch strips. Next place two Velcro dots on opposite ends of each strip, so that when the Velcro strip is manipulated into a circle, the dots connect.

Encourage your child to manipulate the foam strips into circles to make a chain.

You could easily turn this into an educational activity by focusing on sorting the foam links by color or using them to create patterns and/or addition and subtraction problems.

Notes / Tips

Add alphabet or number stickers to the middle of each foam strip for more learning possibilities!

Paper Punching

Materials / Supplies

- Construction paper
- Scrapbook paper
- Paper punches in different shapes
- Hole punch

by **Kristina Couturier**
School Time Snippets
Learn and play today
www.schooltimesnippets.com

How to

This busy bag can be used as a diversion when you need a few minutes to get something done or can be made into a lovely table-top invitation to create activity.

Set out several pieces of construction paper and scrapbook paper and a few artistic paper punches in different shapes.

With those two materials, encourage your child to manipulate the paper punches to create designs in the paper and pieces of "confetti."

Paper-punching is a quick and simple way to work on finger dexterity and hand strength.

Notes / Tips

This busy bag could also be used to work on patterns, counting, and addition! Or get a bit creative and provide your child with contact paper or glue to create a picture with the paper confetti!

Paper Clip Chain

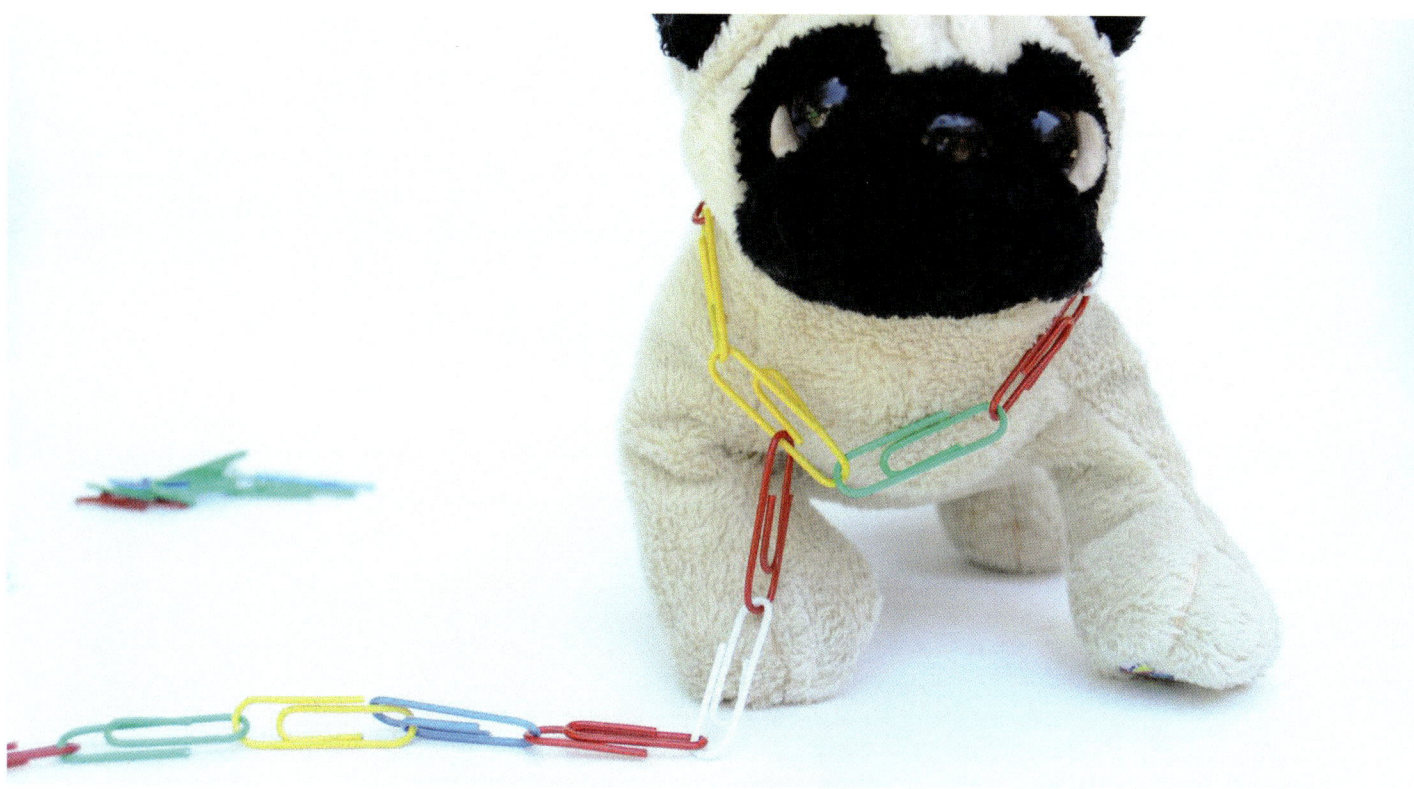

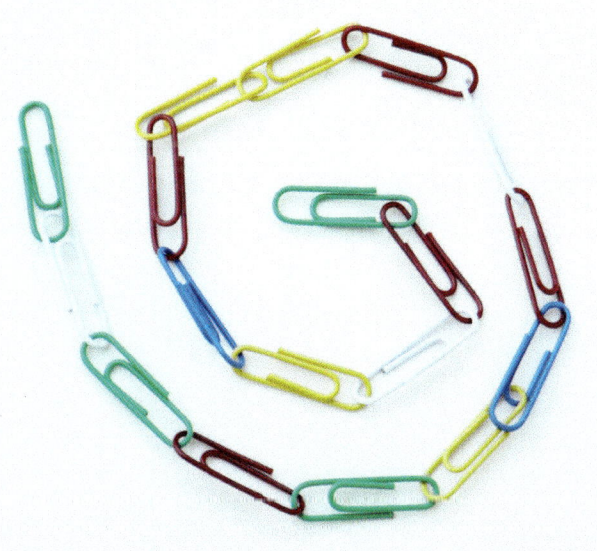

by **Emma Craig**
Our Whimsical Days
Memories in the making
www.ourwhimsicaldays.com

Materials / Supplies

- Paperclips

How to

Adults look at paperclips as more of a means to an end. They keep sheets of paper together, case closed. Kids are more likely to think of them as an activity all on their own.

Paperclip chains make a great busy bag activity because they only require one material. If kids get bored just clipping them together, then try offering a challenge. Who can make the longest chain? Can you make a pattern with colored clips?

They can also make jewelry! Kids will love making paperclip bracelets, necklaces, and even accessories for their stuffed friends. (Here is our toy dog modeling a lovely paper clip leash.)

Notes / Tips

These would make a great "garland" to hang on the Christmas tree using red and green paperclips. A decoration that also helps fine motor skills? Yes, please!

Aluminum Foil Roll

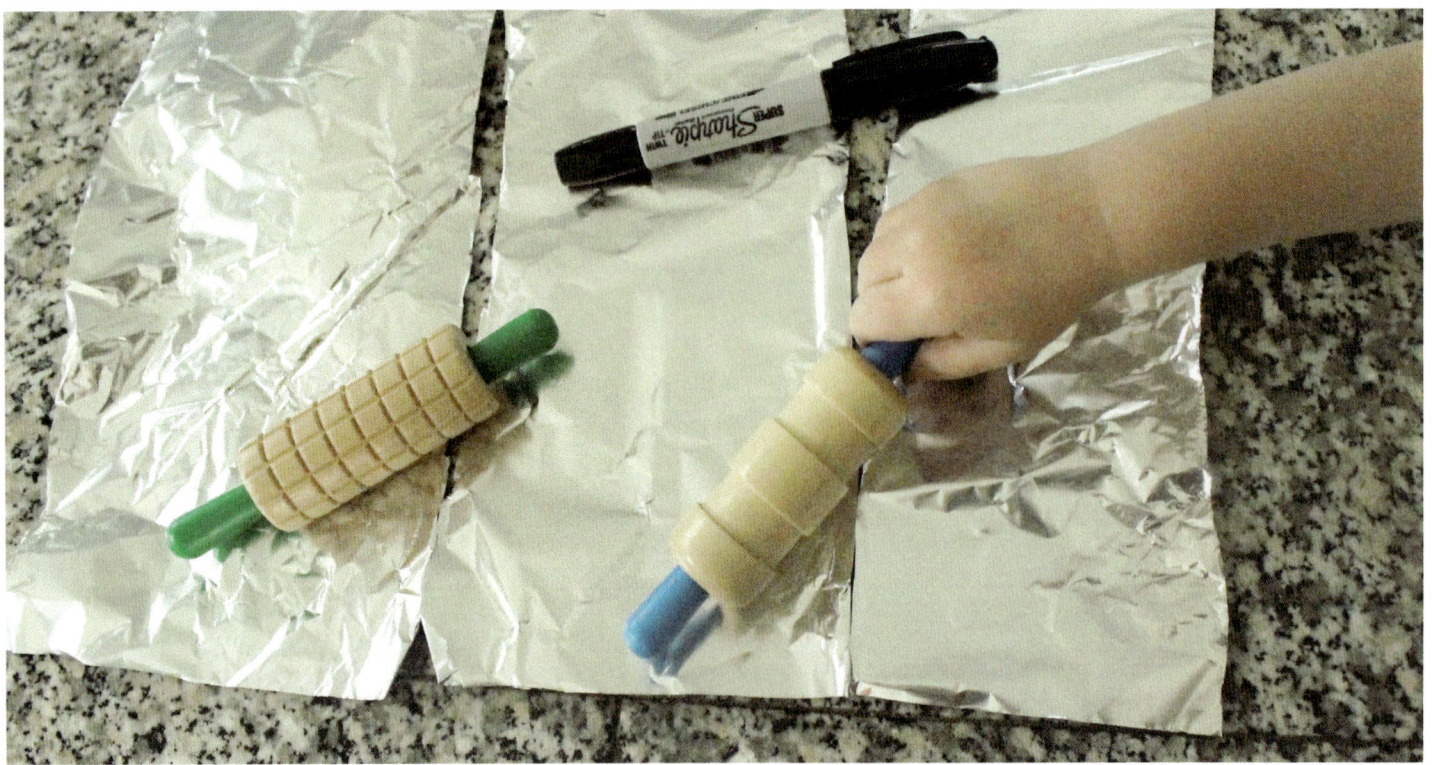

Materials / Supplies

- Aluminum foil
- Several long cylindrical objects (such as writing utensils, small rolling pins, etc.)
- Plastic bag (for storage - optional)

by **Blayne Burke**
House of Burke
Learning and exploring together as a family!
www.houseofburkeblog.com

How to

You would be surprised how exciting unconventional materials can be to little ones. Whenever I go to get the aluminum foil out to wrap up some leftovers, I have little hands reaching out to get a feel of it. Aluminum foil itself, is a great fine motor material. It can be pinched and molded to fit your needs.

For this activity, cut several pieces of aluminum foil and lay them out with several long cylindrical objects. I used a marker and two differently shaped playdough rolling pins. Encourage your little one to put the object at the side of the aluminum foil closest to them. Then, invite them to wrap the foil around the object as tightly as they can, and roll away from them. They should try to roll the object around until the foil strip is gone. They can then repeat this action for the other objects. When you are done, then you can compare the different sizes of the wrapped objects.

This activity gives an intense fine motor workout for tiny fingers. Plus, it gives your child a chance to get their hands on a new and fun material! When they are finished, unwrap the objects, and store in a plastic bag to use again.

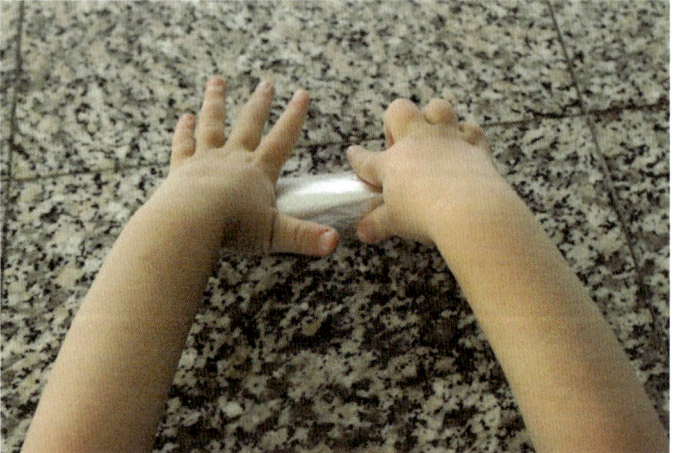

Notes / Tips

Wrap differently shaped objects. Have your child build towers and sculptures by wrapping the tin foil around different shapes and building with them.

Button Sorting

by **Nicolette Roux**
Powerful Mothering
Learning one step at a time
www.PowerfulMothering.com

Materials / Supplies

- Buttons of various shapes and sizes
- Transparent plastic cups
- Tray to contain activity

How to

To prepare the activity, pour the buttons onto the tray. Encourage your child to sort the buttons based on color or by shape.

Do this first by stacking the buttons then introduce the transparent cups to add a new twist on the game.

As your child uses their pincer action to pick these buttons up to transfer and sort the buttons they are strengthening those muscles.

Notes / Tips

My three year old loves this game so much that she will happily sort an entire bag of buttons.

Lacing Beads

by **Devany LeDrew**
Still Playing School
Playing, learning, remembering
www.stillplayingschool.com

Materials / Supplies

- Small plastic strainer
- Lacing cord
- Beads
- Zippered bag

How to

Mini plastic strainers from the dollar store are perfect for this busy bag!

Simply string plastic lacing cord through one hole in the strainer and tie a knot to secure it.

Invite children to thread the cord through the strainer in a stitching pattern. You can also add beads for extra fine motor fun.

Challenge your kids to make patterns and designs as they sew!

Notes / Tips

Use letter beads to invite older children to spell names and other words.

Building with Straws and Play Dough

by **Sarah McClelland**
Little Bins For Little Hands
A Sensory Filled Life
www.littlebinsforlittlehands.com

Materials / Supplies

- Plastic straws
- Play dough
- Scissors (optional)

Notes / Tips

You could draw simple pictures, letters, or shapes on cards and add them to the busy bag for kids who like to have some inspiration to get started. You could also add googly eyes and beads for extra creativity.

How to

When you combine plastic straws and play dough, you get a fun fine motor building activity that is great for quiet time play and learning. The only two items you need for this fine motor busy bag are straws and play dough. If your kids are working on scissor skills, then add a pair of scissors for them to cut the straws into different size lengths. Otherwise, you can pre-cut a variety of sizes. Add the straws and play dough to a bag or box and you are ready to go.

Show your kids how to make play dough balls by rolling chunks of play dough between their hands. Push the straws into the play dough to make all sorts of crazy sculptures, shapes, or letters. There are so many possibilities.

Working with play dough strengthens hand muscles. Holding straws and pushing them into the play dough is great for finger dexterity. Using both hands to steady the straws and play dough, so that another piece can be added, is perfect for hand-eye coordination!

Older kids can build more complex structures while younger kids will enjoy pushing the straws into the play dough. Either way, several important finger grasps are used which will strengthen hands for pencil use later on!

Busy Bags {37}

Threading Washers and Nuts

How to

Here is a terrific fine motor busy box idea that can be set up for multiple ages. Packages of nuts and washers can be bought from hardware stores. The sizes range from quite large to very small, perfect for small hands. I added fun patterned pipe cleaners and then my son decided to add some colored beads.

Although my son knew exactly what to do with this busy box, you can start off the activity by threading several of the items onto the pipe cleaner. Depending on the size of the washers and nuts, you can bend the pipe cleaner at one end to prevent them from slipping off. If you choose large washers and nuts, then you can wrap an end of the pipe cleaner around one to get started and prevent the others from sliding off.

Threading small items encourages kids to use the pincer grasp (thumb and first finger) or the tripod grasp (thumb and first two fingers). These grasps are important for holding pencils. Threading activities like this will strengthen hands and increase finger dexterity.

by **Sarah McClelland**
Little Bins For Little Hands
A Sensory Filled Life
www.littlebinsforlittlehands.com

Materials / Supplies

- Pipe cleaners
- Nuts
- Washers
- Beads (optional)

Notes / Tips

Other ways to incorporate learning into this threading activity would be to create patterns with the washers and nuts. You can also use this activity for one to one counting. If you have matching bolts, then kids could thread on the washers and screw on the nuts.

Rainbow Bubble Wrap Busy Bag

by **Laura Marschel**
Lalymom
Home with two, creativity will brew
www.Lalymom.com

Materials / Supplies

- Bubble wrap
- Permanent markers in red, orange, yellow, green, blue, indigo, and violet (we only had one blue for ours, that is up to you)
- Scissors

How to

Cut a long strip of bubble wrap that is six or seven bubbles wide, depending on how many of the rainbow colors you have.

Use the markers to color the first bubble of each row in the ROYGBIV order.

Place the markers and the strip of bubble wrap into the zipper bag. Invite your child to complete the pattern along all the bubbles. Or hang it in the window as a rainbow suncatcher!

Notes / Tips

Once the marker is dry, your child can pop the bubbles, you can go in rainbow order to reinforce the color order. Be sure to wait until it is dry. Both my kids popped the bubbles and got some color onto their fingers, but it didn't stain once it had dried.

Counting Sticks

How to

Lay out your craft sticks in a row and number them from one to ten. You could write numerals on both sides or you could write numerals on one side and the number words on the other.

Now do the same for the clothespins.

Depending on the age of your child you may like to add color to your craft sticks to help younger children with color matching.

Encourage your child to match up the numbers!

by **Nicolette Roux**
Powerful Mothering
Learning one step at a time
www.PowerfulMothering.com

Materials / Supplies

- 10 jumbo craft sticks
- 10 wooden clothespins
- Black pen
- Color pens (optional)

Notes / Tips

My daughter could not really open clothespins until she was three years old, so this activity might be better suited to older preschool children.

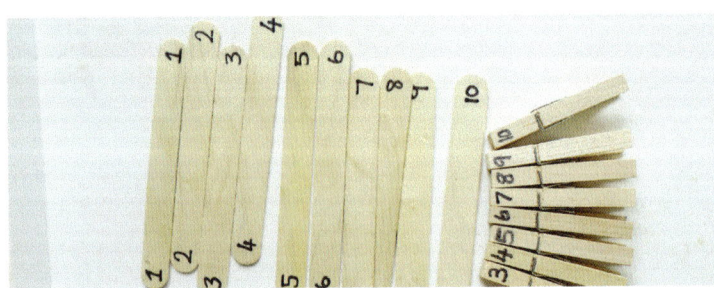

{40} 100 Fine Motor Ideas

Body Part Matching Game

by **Blayne Burke**
House of Burke
Learning and exploring together as a family!
www.houseofburkeblog.com

Materials / Supplies

- Body outline
- Picture of your child
- Glue stick
- Laminator
- Clothespins
- Permanent marker

Notes / Tips

Let your child use their minis to play Simon Says! For example say, "Simon says find your head. Good! Find your arm. Oops, Simon did not say that!"

How to

If your child is interested in learning their body parts with a fun personalized twist, then this activity is for them! This activity can be used with reading age, as well as younger toddlers. For little ones, just call out the name of the body part on each pin.

To make this busy bag, first find a simple body outline. Depending on your child, find an outline that suits them. Print out a picture of your child's face similar in size to the body. Paste it on using the glue stick. If you want, let your child decorate their mini figure to match their favorite outfit. Then run it through a laminator to make sure it is nice and durable! Write the names of the different body parts on the clothespins.

Encourage your little one to exercise their fine motor skills while learning their body parts. Older children will be able to sound out the words and practice new vocabulary while younger children will be able to work on their auditory skills by listening to each of the body parts being called out.

Busy Bags {41}

Sensory

Play Dough Balloons by Georgina, Craftulate

Citrus Scented Salt Tray by Dyan, And Next Comes L

LEGO® Sensory Soup by Dyan, And Next Comes L

Pre-Writing Squish Bag by Sarah, Little Bins For Little Hands

Shape Sorting Sensory Play by Samantha, Stir the Wonder

Life-Size Pom Pom Pit by Kristina, School Time Snippets

Moon Dust Writing Tray by Samantha, Stir the Wonder

Sensory Sound Blocks by Emma, P is for Preschooler

Search and Find Slime by Sarah, Little Bins For Little Hands

Color Sorting on the Light Table by Dyan, And Next Comes L

Taste-Safe Kinetic Sand Play by Blayne, House of Burke

Play Dough Surprise by Devany, Still Playing School

Fine Motor Beach Activities by Laura, Lalymom

Treasure Hunting by Nicolette, Powerful Mothering

Play Dough Balloons

How to

Play dough balloons are a great way to use up slightly "crusty" old play dough or play dough that has had the colors mixed together beyond recognition.

To fill the balloons, roll the dough into tiny logs and feed them into the neck of the balloon. If your child has the patience to do this step, then it makes a bonus fine motor activity!

At first, the little logs will just fall into the balloon – although every now and then you might need to close the opening and shake them down. Then it will start to get a bit trickier and you will need to work the dough down into the balloon so that it attaches to the other pieces of dough, freeing up the neck for more dough.

Keep filling and squishing and try to get as much play dough into the balloon as possible. Then tie a knot in the end.

Children can use these play dough balloons for building finger muscles. They are also perfect for fidgety hands or as a stress toy for adults!

by **Georgina Bomer**
Craftulate
Making. Learning. Fun.
www.craftulate.com

Materials / Supplies

- Balloons
- Play dough

Notes / Tips

Draw silly faces on the balloons with permanent marker to make little characters!

Citrus Scented Salt Tray

by **Dyan Robson**
And Next Comes L
Hyperlexia + Autism + Other Tales of Learning
www.andnextcomesL.com

Materials / Supplies

- Shallow dish or tray
- Table salt
- Liquid watercolors or food coloring
- Citrus essential oils (mandarin orange, lemon, and grapefruit)
- Small resealable bag
- Chopstick (optional)

Notes / Tips

You can substitute sugar for the salt. Try adding glitter to the tray!

How to

Salt trays are a great way to work on mark making and pre-writing skills. They are also great because you can simply use materials from your own kitchen. You can easily transform an ordinary salt tray by adding some colors and scents to boost the sensory experience. We personally love citrus scents at our house so we made a blend of mandarin orange, lemon, and grapefruit in our salt tray. It smelled wonderful!

To make the colored and scented salt, place some salt in a small resealable bag. How much salt you use depends on how big of a dish you use. We used about 1 cup of salt for our salt tray. Next, add a couple squirts of liquid watercolors and 3 drops of essential oils to the bag. Seal the bag and shake the contents until the color is evenly distributed. Kids will enjoy helping with the shaking part! Finally, let the colored salt air dry in the shallow dish before playing with it.

Once dry, the kids can practice drawing shapes, making designs, writing letters and words, etc. by using their fingers or a chopstick to make marks in the salt. Kids who have tactile sensitivities may prefer drawing with a chopstick instead of using their fingers.

Sensory {45}

LEGO® Sensory Soup

by **Dyan Robson**
And Next Comes L
Hyperlexia + Autism + Other Tales of Learning
www.andnextcomesL.com

Materials / Supplies

- Water
- LEGO® bricks
- Kitchen utensils: large spoon, whisk, ladle, bowl, etc.

How to

Water sensory soups are probably the easiest and most loved activities in our house. I love making them and my boys absolutely adore playing with them! All that scooping and pouring is great for encouraging fine motor skills, while also letting the kids engage in imaginary play. You could also add measuring cups and measuring spoons to sensory bins like this LEGO® one to really encourage the exploration of mathematical concepts like volume, measurement, and estimation.

To make this LEGO® sensory soup, simply fill a large bin with water and add a variety of LEGO® bricks. Then add the kitchen utensils and a bowl. That's it! So easy to set up, but great for hours of play.

Notes / Tips

You can create any kind of sensory soup simply by replacing the LEGO® bricks with some other materials like buttons, feathers, straws, mini figurines, etc. You can also try adding liquid watercolors and/or some essential oils to the water to enhance the sensory experience.

Pre-Writing Squish Bag

by **Sarah McClelland**
Little Bins For Little Hands
A Sensory Filled Life
www.littlebinsforlittlehands.com

Materials / Supplies

- Gallon size zipper seal bag
- 16oz bottle of hair gel (any color)
- Googly eyes (mixed sizes)
- Black permanent marker
- Clear packing tape (optional, but advisable!)

Notes / Tips

Instead of drawing directly on the bag, draw on a piece of white paper and place it underneath the bag. You can make letters, numbers, mazes, silly faces, and all types of lines! A squish bag is excellent for building pre-writing skills.

How to

To make a fine motor squish bag, fill a large, clear zipper bag with hair gel. Do not add too much otherwise the objects will not move around well. You could invite your kids to help with this step as squeezing is a great fine motor movement!

Next, add a handful of different sized googly eyes to the bag. You can place them on a tray and have your kids use their fingers or tweezers to transfer them into the bag for additional fine motor work.

Make sure all the air is out of the bag before you seal it. You may want to reinforce the top of the bag with clear packaging tape.

Place the squish bag flat on a counter or table and have your kids work the hair gel around evenly with their fingers. Use a black permanent marker to make different size circles all over the bag.

Invite your kids to use their pointer finger to move the eyes into the circles. They could try to get large eyes into large circles and small eyes into small circles.

Isolating the fingers is great fine motor work. Moving the googly eyes around the bag and into the circles is perfect for improving both hand-eye coordination and visual processing skills.

Shape Sorting Sensory Play

How to

This activity incorporates early math skills such as identifying shapes and sorting, as well as fine motor skills and tactile sensory input. Plus, it is quick and easy to set up!

Fill the bin with black beans and shape buttons. Arrange the bin, muffin tin, and fine motor tools on a table and invite your children to play.

Kids will most likely come up with their own ways to play with the items, but here are some ideas you could suggest:

- Place a different shaped button in each section of the muffin tin and invite the children to sort the buttons into the tin. They can use their fingers or fine motor tools to grab and sort the buttons!
- Use two ice cube trays and make a game of filling the ice cube sections with shape buttons! The first player to fill their tray wins!
- Use the fine motor tools to fill the muffin tin with beans!

by **Samantha Soper-Caetano**
Stir the Wonder
Inspiring Learning
www.stirthewonder.com

Materials / Supplies

- Black beans
- Shape buttons
- Fine motor tools such as tweezers
- Small muffin tin
- Bin or container
- Ice cube tray (optional)
- Number die (optional)

Notes / Tips

You can also turn this shape sorting sensory bin into a simple counting game! Use a number die to determine how many shapes to add to an ice cube tray. Take turns rolling the die. The first player to fill each section of their ice cube tray wins.

100 Fine Motor Ideas

Life-Size Pom Pom Pit

by **Kristina Couturier**
School Time Snippets
Learn and play today
www.schooltimesnippets.com

Materials / Supplies

- Laundry basket (the kind with holes)
- Pom poms
- Tweezers and/or tongs (optional)
- Clothespins (optional)
- Sorting container (optional)

How to

Kids can work on fine motor skills while being surrounded by pom poms! Grab a laundry basket that has holes and simply pour a bag or two of pom poms into the bottom.

Invite your child to climb into this life-size pom pom pit for some fun! We kept the play simple and had fun pushing the pom poms through the holes in the laundry basket. However, you could also use this pom pom pit to talk about colors, size, and numbers.

Add in some tongs, tweezers, or clothespins to grab at the pom poms and provide a container for your child to drop the pom poms into for a sorting extension.

Notes / Tips

An assortment of different sized pom poms works for this activity, but pom poms two inches or bigger are recommended if children under one year old are playing.

Moon Dust Writing Tray

How to

A salt writing tray is a great way to provide tactile sensory input which further enhances the multi-sensory learning and memory of this activity.

To prepare this activity, you will need to make some moon dust, also known as colored salt. Measure about one cup of table salt into a container. Squeeze a little bit of gray tempera paint into the salt and mix it up well. Spread it out on a tray and then let it dry thoroughly in a sunny window. If it gets a little clumpy, then just break it up with your hands.

Next, make an astronaut writing tool. Paint a wooden peg doll with white acrylic paint and let it dry. Then use a black permanent marker to draw hair and a face on it.

Once dry, set up the moon dust in a shallow tray with the astronaut writing tool and invite your child to practice mark making or writing letters in the dust! A quick demonstration might be needed to show your child how to use the writing tray properly.

For children who do not recognize letters yet, encourage different mark making in the salt tray. Try vertical lines, horizontal lines, diagonal lines, wavy lines, zigzag lines, etc. All of these marks will help improve handwriting down the road. Young children can also practice mark making using their index finger.

by **Samantha Soper-Caetano**
Stir the Wonder
Inspiring Learning
www.stirthewonder.com

Materials / Supplies

- Salt
- Gray tempera paint
- Tray
- Wooden peg doll
- White acrylic paint
- Black permanent marker

Notes / Tips

If you have children who recognize letters and have experience with writing, then place some alphabet tactile cards or flashcards next to the tray and encourage them to try writing the different letters in the moon dust!

Sensory Sound Blocks

by **Emma Craig**
Our Whimsical Days
Memories in the making
www.ourwhimsicaldays.com

Materials / Supplies

- Small plastic containers with caps
- Small items that make noise when you shake them
- Packing tape

Notes / Tips

Try playing the "What was that?" games with your preschooler. Have the child close his or her eyes and try to guess which block you are shaking.

How to

Sounds blocks have intrigued me for a while. They are a cute children's toy made out wood or plastic, containing different objects or voice boxes. I thought them a great multisensory toy for my child, but instead of spending the money, I decided to make some of my own. It was very simple!

I purchased several small containers from the Dollar Store, and with the help of my daughter Kay, filled them with sand, beads, buttons, and colored rice. This is what we used, but other objects such as bouncy balls or jacks could work as well. To keep the objects from falling out a.k.a. to childproof them, I sealed the tops with clear packing tape.

My one-year-old niece absolutely loves these homemade sound blocks! Even my six-year-old enjoys shaking and stacking them.

Sensory {51}

Search and Find Slime

How to

This slime is quick and easy to make. Simply mix 1/2 cup of glue and ½ cup of water in one bowl until thoroughly mixed. Pour a 1/2 cup of liquid starch into another bowl. Add glue mixture to starch and stir. You will want to continue mixing with your hand until starch is all gone. Transfer the slime to a clean storage container. Let slime sit for 15 minutes or use right away. The slime will last a few weeks if stored in a sealed container.

For fun, fine motor, and sensory play, mix small objects into the slime. Place the slime on a tray or leave in the container. Have your kids go on a treasure hunt and remove all of the tiny items with their fingers or tweezers.

This slime sensory search will improve finger dexterity as your kids try to pull objects out of the slime. Plus, tactile sensory stimulation is excellent for fine motor development. My son used several different grasps including the pincer and tripod grasp to remove the tiny items. Manipulating the slime is also great hand work. Hunting down the objects is great for improving visual skills!

Don't have time or ingredients to make slime? You can also mix your tiny treasures into a big pile of play dough. Or add them to a bin filled with rice. Any of these tactile sensory play ideas will work on fine motor skills.

by **Sarah McClelland**
Little Bins For Little Hands
A Sensory Filled Life
www.littlebinsforlittlehands.com

Materials / Supplies

- Elmer's Washable Glue (This brand is the recommended glue for consistency.)
- Liquid starch (found in laundry detergent aisle)
- Water
- 2 bowls, a spoon, 1/2 cup measure
- Tiny objects such as LEGO® pieces, Playmobil pieces, beads, gems, google eyes, sequins, and trinkets!
- Container or tray

Notes / Tips

You can make your slime any color. When mixing glue and water together, add liquid food coloring and/or even glitter. You can also use Elmer's Washable Clear Glue to make clear slimes.

Color Sorting on the Light Table

Materials / Supplies

- Light table, light box, or light panel
- Colored translucent plastic tube shots - you can find these at the dollar store
- Colored translucent cocktail stirrers - you can also find these at the dollar store

Notes / Tips

When the kids have finished color matching, use the colored stir sticks to make shapes, letters, or numbers.

by **Dyan Robson**
And Next Comes L
Hyperlexia + Autism + Other Tales of Learning
www.andnextcomesL.com

How to

This light table invitation takes only a few seconds to set up and is extremely appealing to kids because of the added light source. Yet, this activity can be done off of the light table as well. It focuses on color sorting and matching.

Simply set out some tube shots (translucent baskets or trays would work too!) and some cocktail stirrers in corresponding colors. Picking up and transferring the stir sticks is a great fine motor workout, while lining up and inserting the stir sticks into the tube shots is great for developing hand-eye coordination.

Sensory {53}

Taste-Safe Kinetic Sand

How to

We absolutely love kinetic sand! It is such a unique sensory material and has the capacity to be molded while also being fluid. However, kinetic sand is not safe for little ones who are mouthing. Brown sugar is a fabulous edible substitute! You will notice when baking that the properties of brown sugar are very similar to kinetic sand. It can be molded and it can also be fluid. It is even the same color.

Prepare your brown sugar by popping it in the freezer the night before. This step ensures that the brown sugar resists melting between your hands during play. It is best to do this activity in a cool environment. Unlike real kinetic sand, brown sugar will not retain its form if it becomes too warm.

Present your brown sugar sand in a large dish or container. Make sure to provide plastic tweezers, spoons, scoops, cups, etc. so that your little one can work on different fine motor skills while at play. Because the brown sugar becomes a solid when molded, encourage your child to pinch, build, and pack. Let them observe the different properties while they play!

by **Blayne Burke**
House of Burke
Learning and exploring together as a family!
www.houseofburkeblog.com

Materials / Supplies

- Brown sugar
- Large dish or bin
- Tweezers, spoons, scoops

Notes / Tips

This sensory play was created by necessity. Our littlest babe is incredibly oral and sticks EVERYTHING in his mouth. Our oldest never mouthed anything so I was able to easily do all kinds of sensory play with him from a super young age. This activity is suitable for both of them!

Play Dough Surprise

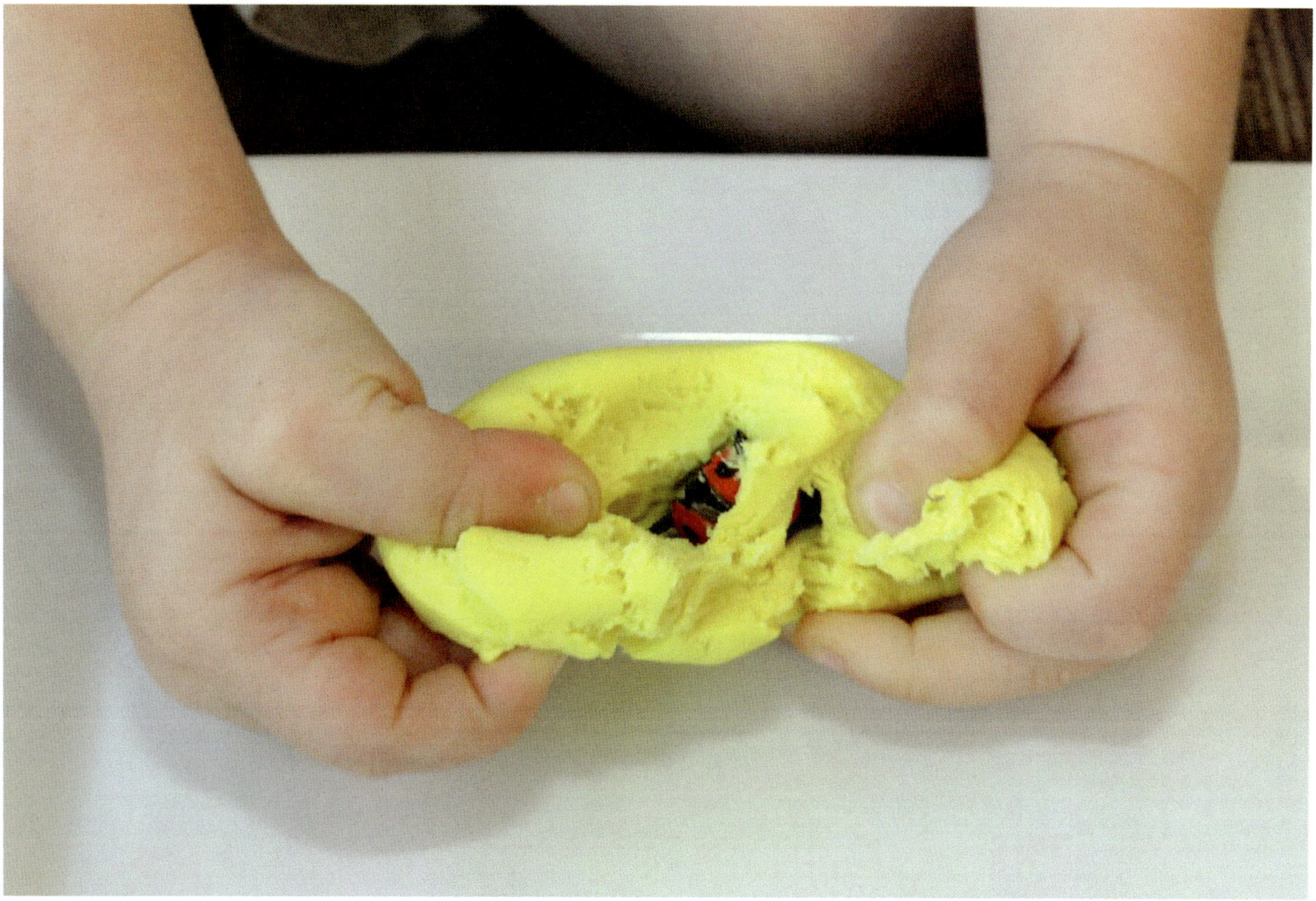

by **Devany LeDrew**
Still Playing School
Playing, learning, remembering
www.stillplayingschool.com

Materials / Supplies

- Play dough
- Small items to hide inside

Notes / Tips

Change this invitation to play for holidays! Choose play dough colors that match the season too. For example, you can hide spider rings in orange and black play dough for Halloween!

How to

Our son is play dough obsessed! I decided to use this interest to add extra fine motor practice to our activities by hiding secret surprises inside the dough.

Gather small items that you have around the house to put inside the play dough. We used tiny animal figures, but you could use buttons, coins, letter magnets, toy cars, or anything that washes well after the activity.

Roll the little items into the play dough balls. We like one color of play dough per item, but that certainly is not necessary. You can use store bought or homemade play dough.

I set the play dough balls on a tray as I explained that there were surprises inside. Our son could not resist digging right in, but you could give clues and guess the contents of each play dough ball with older kids too!

After all the surprises are discovered it would be extra fine motor practice to invite your child to help you wash the small items in soapy water!

Fine Motor Beach Activities

How to

The beach is a sensory haven for kids. Even if you are not a "beach person," try to give your kids exposure to all the opportunities for exploration, sensory experiences, and fine motor skills practice!

Here are some fun ways to encourage fine motor skills development the next time you go to the beach.

- Write or draw in the sand with sea shells.
- Bring cups to fill and spill with water.
- Scoop and fill buckets with sand to build sand castles.
- Dig a moat around your sand castle.
- Shovel sand in lines to spell a name.
- Decorate a sand castle with sea shells and sticks.
- Use a stick to poke dots in wet sand to make a picture.
- Play tic tac toe in the sand.
- Scoop water into a bucket with a shovel.
- See how high sand can be piled up using only hands. Is it easier with wet sand or dry sand?
- Experiment by placing a hand flat on the sand and trying to dig fingers into the sand. Can you do it in wet sand and dry sand?

by **Laura Marschel**
Lalymom
Home with two, creativity will brew
www.Lalymom.com

Materials / Supplies

- A beach
- Sea shells
- Cups
- Buckets
- Shovels
- Sticks

Notes / Tips

If you do not live near a beach and cannot travel to one, then many of these activities will be just as fun in a sand box, an empty area of a garden, or on a hike in the woods.

Treasure Hunting

by **Nicolette Roux**
Powerful Mothering
Learning one step at a time
www.PowerfulMothering.com

Materials / Supplies

- Whipped Cream
- Treasure hunt items such as buttons and plastic shapes

How to

Here is a simple activity that I love because it is taste safe (with the whipped cream instead of shaving cream), which means that even my youngest, who loves to put things in her mouth at ten months old, can even get involved with bigger items in the bin.

Use a shallow dish and scoop some cream in. At first, let the kids place their items on top of the cream in a decorative fashion. Once they are ready, flatten out the cream with a spoon so that the items are now hidden.

Now go on a treasure hunt! The cream is cool and smooth when digging in it.

Notes / Tips

Once the kids have had their fun, add some cornstarch to your cream a little at a time to turn it into a moldable foam dough.

Sensory

Practical Life

Food and Snack Preparation by Georgina, Craftulate

Washing Clothes by Emma, Our Whimsical Days

Busy Tray by Dyan, And Next Comes L

Towel Folding Activity by Samantha, Stir the Wonder

Window Washing Tray by Samantha, Stir the Wonder

Bike Washing by Emma, Our Whimsical Days

Gift Wrapping Invitation to Play by Blayne, House of Burke

Open and Close Treasure Basket by Kristina, School Time Snippets

Silly Sammy Scissors Practice by Laura, Lalymom

Pet Care by Devany, Still Playing School

Making Lemonade by Devany, Still Playing School

Time to Brush! by Laura, Lalymom

Food and Snack Preparation

How to

These fine motor food preparation ideas all work on different skills. Your child will have an extra incentive if they get to eat the food after they have prepared it!

Food in pouches: It is great fine motor practice to unscrew the caps. Plus, the kids have to squeeze the pouches to get every last drop! Bonus activity: let them screw the caps back on!

Cheese sticks and other cheese snacks: Opening snack cheese - especially string cheese – works on pincer grip. I open the package just a little way for my son, then he does the rest.

Hard-boiled egg: It is all too easy to prepare all our kids' food for them, but like, with the cheese above, sometimes it is fun to let them try to do it by themselves! Peeling a hard-boiled egg needs patience as well as excellent fine motor skills.

Cupcake liners: If you are making cupcakes or muffins then ask your child to place the cupcake liners into the tray for you. Those liners can be very fiddly to pull apart from one another!

Think about all the snacks and food you provide and see if you can get your kids to help. Lids and caps to open, plastic food clips to undo, measuring ingredients, foil or plastic-wrap covered items to unwrap, and many more! If your child can use scissors, then they could help with other tasks such as cutting open packages or snipping herbs like chives. These all use a wide range of fine motor skills!

by **Georgina Bomer**
Craftulate
Making. Learning. Fun.
www.craftulate.com

Materials / Supplies

- Snacks and food that require simple preparation

Notes / Tips

Activity progression: As your child gets older, you could even introduce a kid-friendly knife, with careful adult supervision, of course!

Washing Clothes

by **Emma Craig**
Our Whimsical Days
Memories in the making
www.ourwhimsicaldays.com

Materials / Supplies

- Clothespins
- Liquid soap (we use the last dregs from a shampoo or laundry detergent bottle)
- Clothes
- Bucket
- Water
- String or rope to hang up as a clothesline

Notes / Tips

What else can your child find to hang on the clothesline? Leaves, artwork, shoes? Go exploring for new things to clip on!

How to

Gather some small, easy to manage clothing. We used doll clothes and facecloths because they would be easier to handle. Add some water to the bucket (let your child use the spray hose if you dare!) and then let them squeeze in the soap. We like to add water to the bottle to get the remains of the almost-empty bottle out, shake it, and then pour it into the bucket.

Younger kids might need to be shown how to slosh the article of clothing in the soapy water and then wring it to get the extra water out. This task is tougher for toddlers and early preschoolers than it sounds, but that is what the practice is for!

After wringing out the clothes, hang up the washed articles with the clothespins so that they can dry. My daughter defeated this purpose by pouring the rest of the soapy water onto the clothes. Oh well, pouring is also good for fine motor practice!

Busy Tray

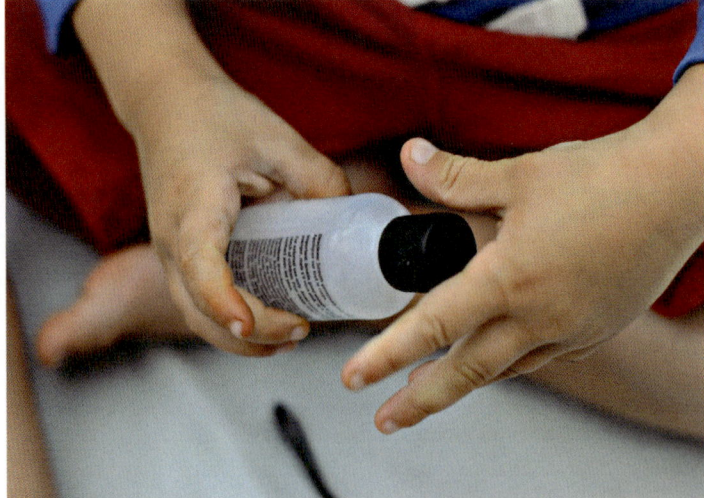
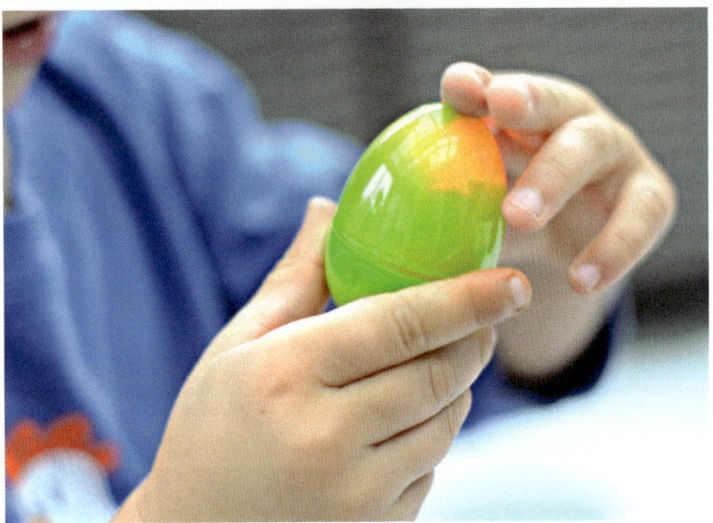

How to

My youngest son has always been interested in playing with real life objects like keys, locks, and flashlights. This practical life skills busy tray is a perfect way to let kids openly explore these types of objects.

This tray uses everyday objects that kids can twist, pull, push, and open. For our tray, I used: a pen keychain that twists to open, an empty lotion bottle (lid can be opened and/or twisted off), a plastic egg, a finger light (has a switch to turn it off and on), a flashlight, a lock and keys, and a velcro keychain that also had a small carabiner clip (velcro is great for encouraging fine motor skills!).

The twisty pen keychain was easily my son's favorite part. He literally sat for 10-15 minutes just twisting and untwisting the pen. He also enjoyed playing with the empty lotion bottle by twisting the lid off and trying to put some of the other objects inside. Additionally, he tried to connect some of the different objects together using the keychains and the strap of the flashlight.

by **Dyan Robson**
And Next Comes L
Hyperlexia + Autism + Other Tales of Learning
www.andnextcomesL.com

Materials / Supplies

- Tray
- Various everyday objects from around your house

Notes / Tips

Before creating this tray, do a scavenger hunt with the kids. Write down a list of objects on a piece of paper and let the kids find the items for the tray.

Towel Folding Activity

by **Samantha Soper-Caetano**
Stir the Wonder
Inspiring Learning
www.stirthewonder.com

Materials / Supplies

- Small face towels
- Flat surface
- Small basket (optional)

Notes / Tips

Start with folding square face towels and then progress to practicing with larger hand and bath towels. Make sure to offer demonstrations for each towel size.

How to

Learning to fold towels is an important practical life task. Not only will it help children learn to take care of themselves as they get older, but it will also help parents accomplish household chores. Children as young as two or three years old can learn to help fold towels and clothes. Plus, they will love practicing with this simple Montessori-inspired practical life activity. It is so simple to set up and you already have what you need, so there is no additional cost.

Gather several face towels in a small basket. Invite your child to the table, floor or other flat surface, and demonstrate how to fold a small face towel.

Make sure to verbalize step by step instructions as you demonstrate. For example, you could say: "Smooth the towel out flat, then fold it in half, and fold it in half again. Then stack it neatly in a pile."

Allow your child as much time as they need to practice folding the face towels and offer encouragement when needed. Remember, the main Montessori principle is: "Follow the lead of the child."

Practical Life {63}

Window Washing Tray

How to

Young kids love helping out around the house! So why not give them their own window washing supplies and demonstrate a real practical life skill?! This simple activity tray is great for practicing fine motor skills and kids will enjoy washing windows over and over again! Just follow these instructions to get started.

First, mix up a homemade window washing solution in the spray bottle. A simple solution of half white vinegar, half water with a few drops of pleasantly scented essential oil works great and is safe for young children to use.

Next, set up a tray with a spray bottle of homemade window cleaner and a wash cloth. A window squeegee is also a great tool to add to the tray.

When your child becomes interested in using the tray, demonstrate how to spray the cleaner all over the window and wipe clean with the wash cloth. Then allow the child to clean as many windows as they like!

by **Samantha Soper-Caetano**
Stir the Wonder
Inspiring Learning
www.stirthewonder.com

Materials / Supplies

- Spray bottle
- Homemade cleaning solution or just water
- Wash cloth
- Tray

Notes / Tips

Squeezing a spray bottle as well as holding a cloth to wipe is a great fine motor strengthening workout for little hands!

Bike Washing

by **Emma Craig**
Our Whimsical Days
Memories in the making
www.ourwhimsicaldays.com

Materials / Supplies

- Bike (scooter, tricycle, even a yard chair will work!)
- Bucket
- Soap
- Sponge

Notes / Tips

Use washable paint to add color to the bike first. Painting on such a unique canvas will have a great novelty factor and give a target for all that cleaning. No need to worry as the washable paint washes right off!

How to

Here is a wonderful warm weather activity to cool off AND hone fine motor skills! And the bike might just get clean too - no promises!

Set out the bike (or other item) that needs to be cleaned far away from whatever you would prefer to stay dry. You'll appreciate this tip when the hose comes into play. Trust me.

Fill up the bucket with water and squirt in some soap. Then mix it up to make it nice and sudsy. Your child will know what to do with the sponge. Encourage them to slosh it in the soapy water and wring out the excess. Then stand back because it is cleaning time!

When the bike is good and soapy, bring out the hose. Let them rinse away all the bubbles and revel in the successful completion of their task.

Last step: take that sparkling bike for a test ride!

Gift Wrapping Invitation to Play

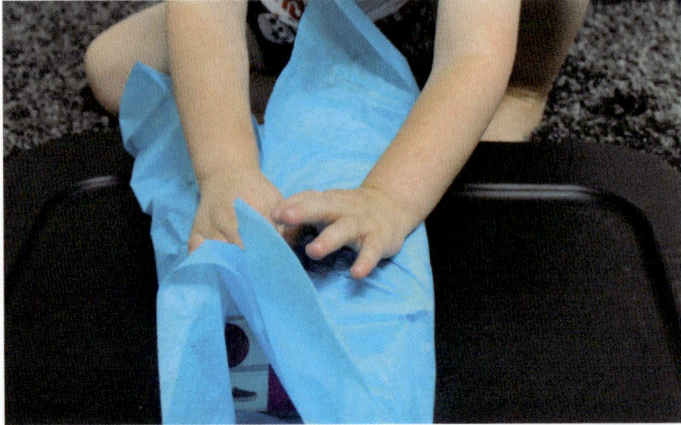

How to

Wrapping gifts is one of my favorite ways to get kids involved in events. Even young toddlers can assist in getting the gift wrapping done for their friend's birthday parties or for various holidays. Wrapping presents involves fine motor skills like folding, taping, ripping, and pinching. It also involves problem solving skills, hand-eye coordination, and helps foster social skills.

To set up the gift wrapping invitation to play, gather four to five objects from around your house that are regular in shape. Items like books or shoeboxes work perfectly! Choose a couple different wrapping mediums. A combination of tissue paper and gift wrap work great. Tissue paper is a great warm up material to regular gift wrap because you do not need to fold it precisely. Pre-cut the paper so that it is ready for your little one to use. Put the tape out with the rest of the materials.

Encourage your little one to select their object to wrap. Demonstrate how to accurately wrap, and then allow them to go at it on their own. If they cannot rip the tape on their own yet, then provide them with pre-ripped pieces.

When they are finished wrapping all of their objects, let them open them on their own. Opening gifts works a whole different set of skills!

by **Blayne Burke**
House of Burke
Learning and exploring together as a family!
www.houseofburkeblog.com

Materials / Supplies

- 4-5 household objects
- Tissue paper
- Gift wrap
- Tape

Notes / Tips

Have your little one create their own wrapping paper with crayons and markers. Then they can wrap gifts for their friends and relatives!

Open and Close Treasure Basket

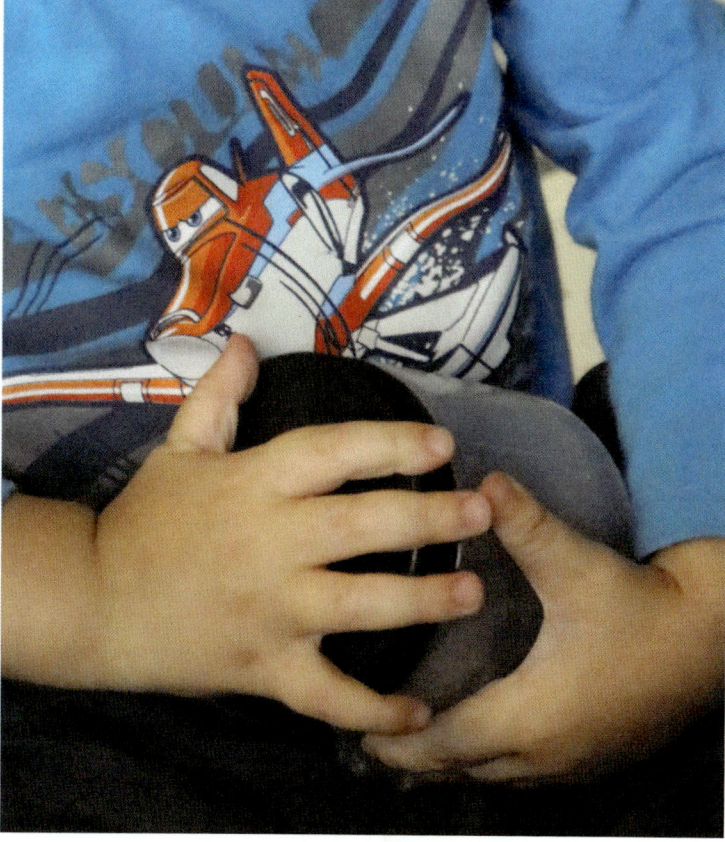

by **Kristina Couturier**
School Time Snippets
Learn and play today
www.schooltimesnippets.com

Materials / Supplies

- Basket or tray
- Spice container
- Wallet
- Drawstring bag
- Jewelry box

Notes / Tips

For a fun variation, hide a snack in each container for some extra motivation to open each item! If you do not have a variety of jars available, then find an old purse with zippers and clasps to manipulate instead.

How to

Gather several materials that require twisting, pulling, manipulating of some sort to open. Here are some examples of what we used:

- An empty spice container that has to be twisted open.
- A folded wallet that has to be pulled apart and contains a zipper pocket.
- Two empty snack containers: one with a twist-top lid and one with a flip top lid.
- A drawstring bag that needs to be pulled apart to open.
- A jewelry box that is held together by magnet strips.
- A small container that you find in a toy vending machine.

Place the assortment of containers in a large basket and encourage your child to open each one.

Practical Life {67}

Silly Sammy Scissors Practice

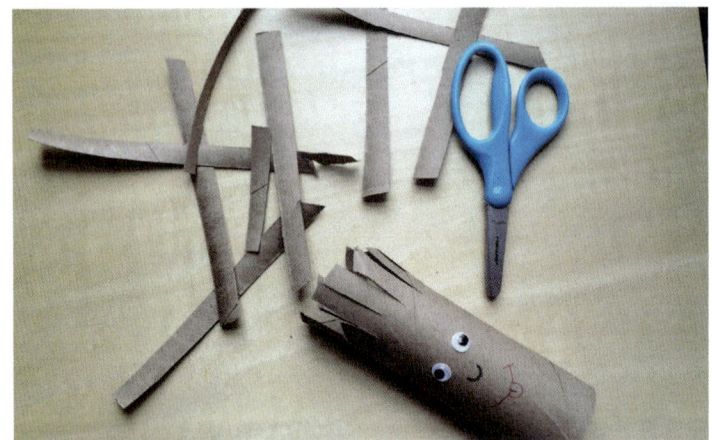

How to

I'm calling this guy Sammy Scissors, but you could call him Harry Haircut, Chris Cuts, Stevie Snips-a-Lot…. encourage your child to be creative and creative silly names for him.

This fun, easy scissors practice activity can be done over and over again with something right out of your recycle bin! Cardboard is a bit thicker than paper of course, so it will be a little harder to cut through. Make sure your child has had experience with cutting paper before moving up to cardboard.

Add googly eyes and draw a face towards the bottom of the cardboard roll. Use your scissors to cut long lines straight down towards the face, all around the roll.

Next, all you need to do is ask your child to give him a haircut! Hooray! Super fun!

by **Laura Marschel**
Lalymom
Home with two, creativity will brew
www.Lalymom.com

Materials / Supplies

- Safety scissors
- Cardboard tube
- Marker
- 2 googly eyes (optional)

Notes / Tips

Draw straight or wiggly lines down the tube and invite your older child to cut on the lines to create the hair. This activity would be fun for an older sibling to create for a younger sibling or to do as a quiet activity alone.

Pet Care

by **Devany LeDrew**
Still Playing School
Playing, learning, remembering
www.stillplayingschool.com

Materials / Supplies

- Pets
- Pet food
- Dishes
- Brush

Notes / Tips

If you do not own a pet, then you could pet sit for a friend or relative or visit a local pet shelter in order to let your children practice caring for an animal!

How to

In many homes pets are members of the family! Here are ways your kids can help take care of animals while practicing fine motor skills at the same time. An adult should always be present to model and praise positive behavior from both the child and the pet.

- Keep your pet food in an airtight container that your child can open and close.
- Explain about how much food to put in the pet's dish at a time. Your child can use a scoop to portion out the food or practice pouring straight from the container. Both are great for fine motor practice!
- Invite your child to wash and fill your pet's water dish too!
- Allow your child to practice appropriately brushing your pet.
- If your pet wears a collar, then your child can practice clipping a leash on and off it for walks.
- Open and close treat containers and feed them to the pet when appropriate.
- Practice tricks with the pet (if applicable) like "Shake hands!"

Practical Life

Making Lemonade

How to

Lemonade is a refreshing treat that can be made with your child as they work on fine motor skills. Invite your child to do as many of the following steps as they can at their developmental level and age.

Begin by washing the lemons. Gently roll the fruit on a table or counter with your hands to soften the lemons so you will get the most juice (and squeeze in extra work with those little hands and wrists)!

Cut the lemons in half. I score the lemons to get them started then allow our kids to finish cutting them with a child-safe knife.

Juice the lemons with a citrus juicer. If you do not have one, then you can also use your hands. Just watch for any seeds that may fall in. Scoop them out with a spoon.

Pour the lemon juice into a pitcher of water. We used one cup of water per lemon. Stir.

Add sugar slowly. Stir and taste as you go to get the perfect sweetness for your liking! We used 1/2 cup of sugar with the juice of 3 lemons and 3 cups of water.

Invite your child to pour the lemonade into glasses over ice. Smaller pitchers with less liquid are easier for kids to pour independently.

Cheers, drink, and enjoy!

by **Devany LeDrew**
Still Playing School
Playing, learning, remembering
www.stillplayingschool.com

Materials / Supplies

- Lemons
- Child safe knife
- Citrus juicer
- Spoon
- Pitcher
- Water
- Sugar
- Measuring cup
- Drinking glasses
- Ice

Notes / Tips

In the winter, hot chocolate is another delicious treat that can be made, served, and enjoyed with your child for fine motor fun!

Time to Brush!

by **Laura Marschel**
Lalymom
Home with two, creativity will brew
www.Lalymom.com

Materials / Supplies

- One Time to Brush! Printable
- Dry erase markers or dry erase crayons
- Spare toothbrush
- Sheet protector or laminator

Notes / Tips

If you have several colors of markers, then talk about what kinds of foods could make your teeth those colors. You could take turns "feeding" the mouth food and coloring the teeth before your clean them off again.

How to

Place the Time to Brush! sheet into a sheet protector or laminate it.

Set out your dry erase markers or dry erase crayons and show your child how to draw on the teeth. Explain that these teeth must have just finished eating and they really need to be cleaned!

Use the spare toothbrush to clean the teeth! Your child can draw more food on and clean it off as many times as he or she wishes!

Show how the right set of teeth match up with the smiling teeth and if necessary open your own mouth to show the shape of your teeth.

When you are done with the activity head right into the bathroom and practice the real deal!

Early Learning

Color Size Match Activity by Georgina, Craftulate

Peeling Tape Letters Pre-Writing Activity by Dyan, And Next Comes L

Button Music Theory Art by Dyan, And Next Comes L

Name Recognition with Clothespegs by Kristina, School Time Snippets

ABC Fish Matching by Samantha, Stir the Wonder

Name Bracelet by Nicolette, Powerful Mothering

Counting Ants Sensory Game by Samantha, Stir the Wonder

Count and Stack Game by Emma, Our Whimsical Days

Crumpled Paper ABC Basketball by Kristina, School Time Snippets

Kitchen Science Experiment by Sarah, Little Bins For Little Hands

Rainbow Ball by Devany, Still Playing School

Patterning Activity by Sarah, Little Bins For Little Hands

Jar Lid Busy Box by Emma, Our Whimsical Days

Play Dough Pinch & Roll Counting Game by Laura, Lalymom

Object Trace by Nicolette, Powerful Mothering

Smashing ABC Moon Rocks by Samantha, Stir the Wonder

Color Size Match Activity

How to

This activity works on size and color matching as well as fine motor skills! Cut a rectangle from each color of card. Do not make them too big otherwise you will not be able to reach to the center with the paper punches. Use different sizes of paper punches to cut holes from each piece of card.

Tape a sheet of clear contact paper to a wall or window, sticky side out. Place all of the cards onto the contact paper.

Provide your child with the punched-out shapes and ask them to match them to the holes on the cards.

This activity can be tailored to any theme simply by using different colors of card, different shapes of card, and/or different paper punch shapes. Perhaps pastel colored card and flower shapes for Easter or spring. Leaves and red/orange/brown card for a fall version. Or hearts with pink and red paper for Valentine's Day.

by **Georgina Bomer**
Craftulate
Making. Learning. Fun.
www.craftulate.com

Materials / Supplies

- Colored card
- Scissors
- Paper punches in various sizes
- Clear contact paper (sticky paper)
- Tape

Notes / Tips

This activity would be lovely for an older sibling to make for a younger one. The older child can develop hand strength by operating the paper punches while the younger child works on pincer grip and hand-eye coordination as they place each punched-out shape.

Peeling Tape Letters Pre-Writing Activity

by **Dyan Robson**
And Next Comes L
Hyperlexia + Autism + Other Tales of Learning
www.andnextcomesL.com

Materials / Supplies

- Tape - masking tape, painter's tape, or washi tape work best
- Marker

Notes / Tips

Try this activity on the light table using washi tape. Or try doing this activity on a vertical surface like a mirror or window.

How to

Kids love tape. Well, at least my kids do. Tape also happens to be a great way for kids to work on fine motor skills. This simple pre-writing letter activity encourages kids to practice letter formation by peeling the tape in the order and direction that you would write the letters themselves.

To make the letters, I ripped pieces of tape and labeled them with a number and a direction based on how to correctly write the letters. Then I layered the tape in reverse order. That means, I placed the tape with number three first and then placed step two next and then finally step one. If you do not put them on a surface like a table or counter in reverse order, then the kids will accidentally peel the entire letter off in one step. You want the kids to peel the letter one strip of tape at a time.

Then it is time to peel! Encourage your kids to follow the numbers and arrows for guidance on how to peel the letters.

Button Music Theory Art

How to

Squeezing glue is a perfect fine motor workout for kids! And there is plenty of glue that went into this art project. Meanwhile, the kids are exploring and learning about music theory. Concepts like music notes, lines and spaces, composition, treble and bass clefs, reading music, and stemming can all be discussed while the kids create.

For this art project, the kids just need to add dabs of glue to different spots on the staff. Then add the colorful buttons. Once the buttons have been placed on the staff, encourage the kids to draw stems for the different notes using black pencil crayons.

If your kids can already read music or are just starting to learn to read music, then they can add extra details like treble and bass clefs, dynamic markings, accents, staccatos, etc. They can also practice identifying the notes that they created with buttons.

by **Dyan Robson**
And Next Comes L
Hyperlexia + Autism + Other Tales of Learning
www.andnextcomesL.com

Materials / Supplies

- Buttons
- Glue
- Black pencil crayons
- Large blank sheet music

Notes / Tips

You can find free extra large blank sheet music for this project by searching for it on Google or you can hand-draw black lines on a blank piece of paper.

Name Recognition with Clothespegs

by **Kristina Couturier**
School Time Snippets
Learn and play today
www.schooltimesnippets.com

Materials / Supplies

- Clothespegs (one for each letter of child's name)
- Alphabet stickers
- Small empty shoebox
- Painter's tape
- Permanent marker

How to

A great alternative to using clothespins is to use clothespegs! For this name recognition activity with a fine motor twist, place a letter sticker on a separate clothespeg spelling out your child's name. You could also just use a permanent marker instead of stickers. Write the same letters on a piece of painter's tape and tape it to the side of a shoe box.

Now encourage you child to match the letter on the clothespeg to the letter on the shoe box and slide the clothespeg onto the box.

Continue until all the clothespegs have been placed in the correct order onto the box.

Notes / Tips

A variation of this activity would be to use clothespins. Alternatively, you could also use this activity to practice number recognition or literacy concepts such as sight words.

Early Learning

ABC Fish Matching

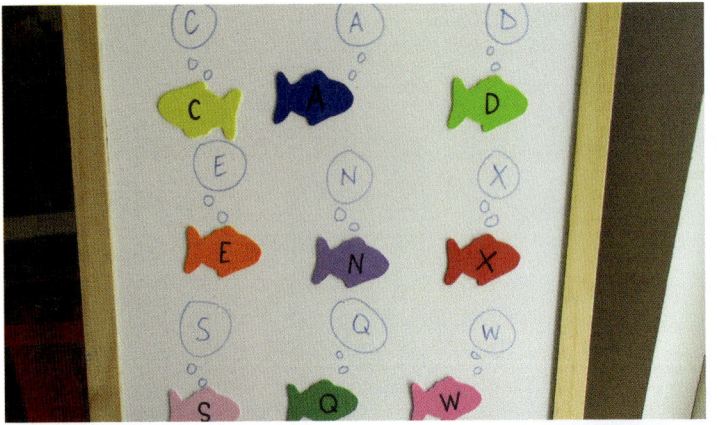

How to

This fine motor activity takes a little prep time for the teacher or parent. Once the supplies have been gathered follow these instructions to set up this activity.

Trace the fish pattern onto the craft foam using a pencil. Make as many as needed, using different colors. Cut out the foam fish using scissors.

Use a permanent marker to write letters on the fish. Write as many as needed for the kids to review. It can be all the letters of the alphabet or just a selection.

On the window or whiteboard use a dry erase marker to draw bubbles and write the corresponding letters in them.

Set out the fish in a bowl and a small spray bottle with water next to the activity and invite your child to play the matching game.

To play the game, kids will select a fish from the bowl, find the matching letter bubble, spray the bubble with water, and stick the corresponding fish to the whiteboard or window. Preschoolers will have fun reviewing the alphabet as they work on strengthening fine motor muscles with the spray bottle!

by **Samantha Soper-Caetano**
Stir the Wonder
Inspiring Learning
www.stirthewonder.com

Materials / Supplies

- Colorful craft foam
- Fish stencil or cookie cutter
- Pencil
- Scissors
- Whiteboard or window
- Spray bottle
- Permanent marker
- Dry erase marker

Notes / Tips

Only half fill the spray bottle with water. If it is too full, then children might have a hard time holding it. Keep a small towel handy to wipe up any dripping water.

Name Bracelet

by **Nicolette Roux**
Powerful Mothering
Learning one step at a time
www.PowerfulMothering.com

Materials / Supplies

- Beads
- Alphabet beads
- Elastic thread

Notes / Tips

You could also make name necklaces!

How to

Learning to recognize and spell their name is a skill that your child needs. With this activity, they work on fine motor skills, get some spelling practice, and receive a snazzy new bracelet in the end!

Measure out the elastic thread on the wrist of your child, leaving a bit extra to tie a knot.

Lay out their name in beads for them to thread on. Tie a bead to the end of the thread to stop other beads falling off, then invite your child to thread the rest of the beads.

After they have finished, tie two knots to secure the bracelet, trim the edges, and push a bead over the knot to hide it.

Counting Ants Sensory Game

How to

This simple game has a lot of benefits for preschoolers. The dirt in the bin offers tactile sensory input for kids who enjoy touching different textures. Using the tweezers is a fun way for kids to work on building fine motor strength and hand-eye coordination. And by placing the ants in individual ice cube squares, preschoolers can practice counting and learn to understand one-to-one correspondence.

Cover the bottom of a plastic bin with a layer of potting soil. Place enough mini plastic ants in the bin to fill each space of your ice cube trays.

Arrange your bin of ants, tweezers or other fine motor tools, ice cube trays and die on a table in an inviting way.

Invite the children to play with the tweezers or other fine motor tools and fill the ice cube trays with ants!

To play the game, players take turns to roll a die and use tweezers to pick up that number of ants. They then place the ants one-by-one into the squares of the ice cube tray. The first player to fill their ice cube tray is the winner!

Use two dice and add the numbers to make the math game more challenging for advanced learners.

by **Samantha Soper-Caetano**
Stir the Wonder
Inspiring Learning
www.stirthewonder.com

Materials / Supplies

- Potting soil
- Mini plastic ants
- Jumbo tweezers, or other fine motor tools
- Ice cube trays
- Die

Notes / Tips

Younger children can practice the pincer grasp by using their fingers to pick up the ants and place them in the ice cube tray.

{80} 100 Fine Motor Ideas

Count and Stack Game

by **Emma Craig**
Our Whimsical Days
Memories in the making
www.ourwhimsicaldays.com

Materials / Supplies

- Blocks
- Die

Notes / Tips

If you do not have blocks available, then try something else! You can make the game more or less challenging by using pool noodle blocks, coins, bottle caps, or paper cups. If you can stack it, then try it!

How to

This super-simple game is perfect for kids who like to stack items then knock them down. It also has a little math and fine motor practice thrown in!

Player one rolls the die. If they roll a 3, then that player takes three blocks and stacks them up in a tower. Then it is the second player's turn to do the same.

The game ends when someone's tower collapses or you run out of blocks, whichever comes first. And the grand finale consists of all the players knocking their towers to the ground.

Crumpled Paper ABC Basketball

How to

Your active child will love this basketball game with a fine motor twist!

Cut several pieces of paper into small squares. With a marker, write a letter on each piece of paper and spread them out all over the floor.

Call out a letter and encourage your child to find it. Once the letter has been found, have your child crumple the piece of paper into a ball and shoot it into the hoop!

Continue playing until all the letters have been found and thrown into the hoop.

Practice un-crumpling the paper and then play all over again!

by **Kristina Couturier**
School Time Snippets
Learn and play today
www.schooltimesnippets.com

Materials / Supplies

- Kid size basketball hoop
- Paper
- Marker
- Scissors

Notes / Tips

Try this fun game for number recognition, colors, or shapes. There are so many possible variations!

Kitchen Science Experiment

by **Sarah McClelland**
Little Bins For Little Hands
A Sensory Filled Life
www.littlebinsforlittlehands.com

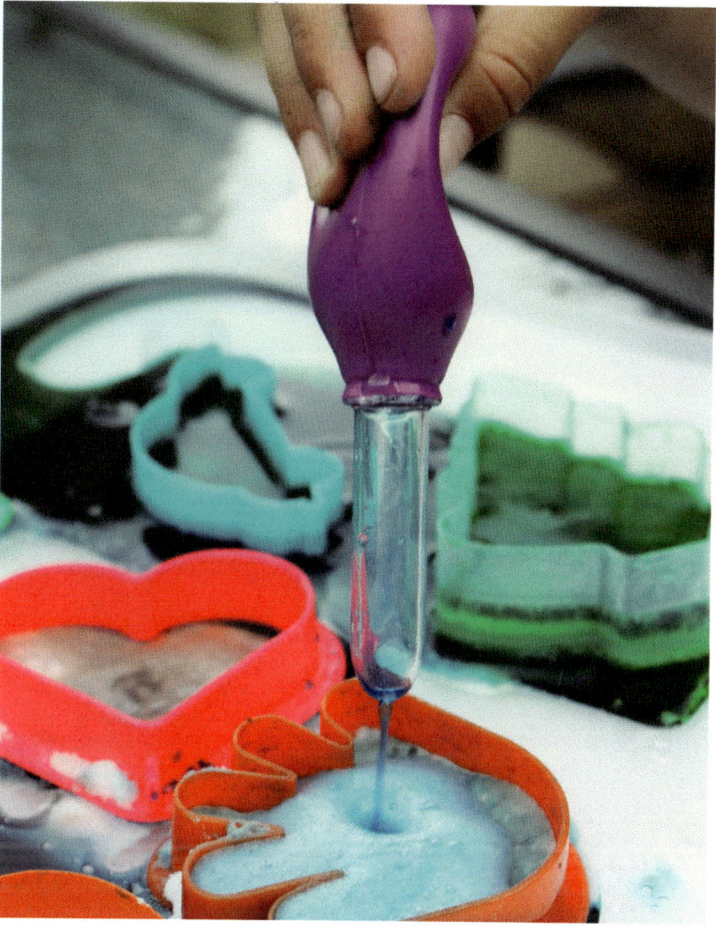

Materials / Supplies

- Baking soda
- Vinegar
- Food coloring
- Cookie cutters
- Cookie sheet or plastic tray
- Small spoon and bowl for baking soda
- Eye droppers
- Small container for vinegar

Notes / Tips

Change the cookie cutters for the different seasons and holidays. We have done themed trays for Halloween, Christmas, Valentine's Day, and 4th of July! Use letter, number, and shapes cookie cutters for early learning!

How to

To set up this fine motor kitchen science activity, all you need to do is open up your pantry! Use any assortment of cookie cutters you like. Even mason jar lids work. Pour baking soda into a bowl and pour vinegar into a container. Place your cookie cutters on your tray. Depending on the skill level of the child, you can fill the cookie cutters with baking soda or let your child use a small spoon for fine motor practice.

When filled, let your child squeeze drops of food coloring into the cookie cutters. This step is a great opportunity to talk about color mixing and adding the appropriate drops of primary colors to make secondary colors. Plus, it works the fingers and encourages control. When you are finished with the color adding, grab an eye dropper and the vinegar container. Have your child squeeze the eye dropper full of vinegar into a baking soda and color filled cookie cutter. Watch the awesome fizzing and bubbling action as well as the color mixing. Repeat over and over!

Rainbow Ball

How to

Scarves in a ball create an irresistible fine motor game for kids. We made it even more interesting by adding all the colors of the rainbow into our play.

Stuff the colored scarves into the ball. You can play several different ways, such as:
- Kids can pass the ball to each other. Each child pulls a scarf from the ball and names the color.
- You could sort the scarves into color coordinating baskets or boxes when they are removed.
- Challenge older children to remove the color you name or take out the colors in rainbow order!

by **Devany LeDrew**
Still Playing School
Playing, learning, remembering
www.stillplayingschool.com

Materials / Supplies

- Oball
- Rainbow scarves

Notes / Tips

My kids loved naming the colors then tossing the scarves up into the air for extra fun!

Patterning Activity

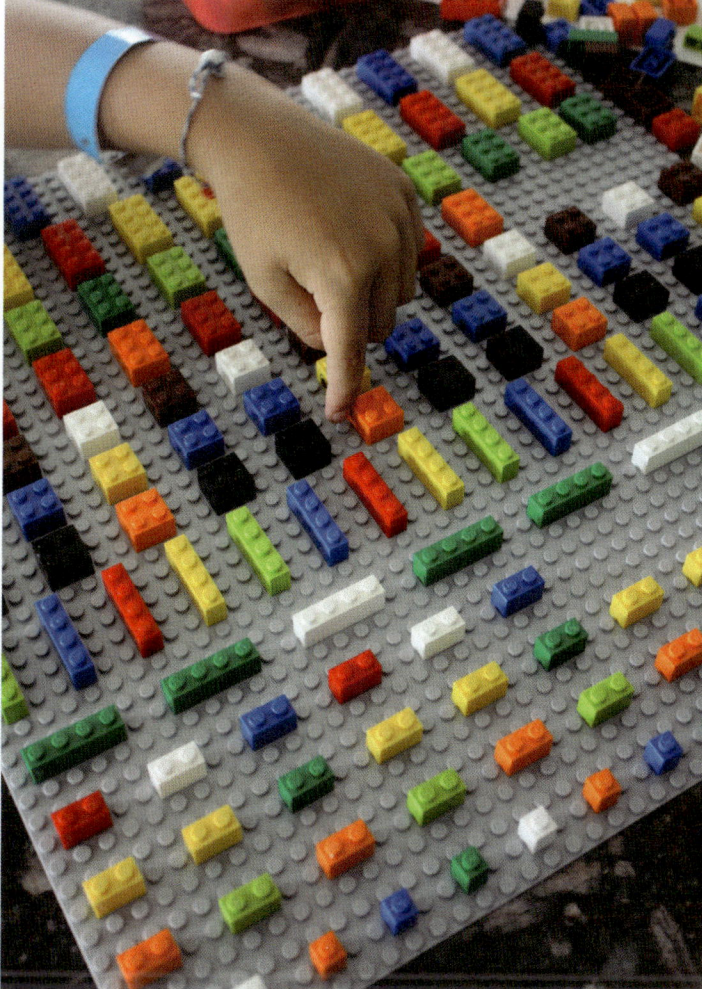

by **Sarah McClelland**
Little Bins For Little Hands
A Sensory Filled Life
www.littlebinsforlittlehands.com

Materials / Supplies

- Large LEGO® baseplate (or similar style building plate)
- LEGO® bricks in a variety of sizes (or similar style building bricks)

Notes / Tips

There are many ways you can vary this fine motor patterning activity. For example, kids can design their own patterns to practice color recognition and counting.

How to

LEGO® bricks are great for working on fine motor skills. Kids love to build with them. The small sizes are perfect for strengthening fingers, improving finger dexterity, and improving hand-eye coordination!

This activity is so simple, but filled with lots of early learning possibilities. I used a large baseplate for our fine motor patterning activity. On the left hand side of the board, I created a pattern for my son to continue across the board. I chose AB, AAB, ABB, ABCD, AABB, and ABA patterns for models.

I started off using large bricks to create the patterns. I gradually chose smaller and smaller bricks as I went down the side of the board. I made two rows of patterns for each brick size for extra practice. The final row consisted of 1x1 size bricks. Make sure to have a container of the right size bricks and colors ready to go. My son's task was to work on his fine motor skills by placing the right bricks in the right order.

Early Learning

Jar Lid Busy Box

by **Emma Craig**
Our Whimsical Days
Memories in the making
www.ourwhimsicaldays.com

How to

Baby jar lids offer some great fine motor skills practice - stacking, tossing, even just picking them up to chew on! This quick activity that I put together builds on my one year old niece's love of dropping things into containers and then emptying them again.

I found a box with a lid and cut random rectangles with a utility knife. I made them different sizes for more of a challenge. It ended up looking like a face, but I promise that was not intentional! I then added glitter tape to the edges because...well, it just looked like it needed a little pizzazz! Then baby can try pushing the lids through the slots.

Materials / Supplies

- Sturdy cardboard box
- Baby jar lids
- Craft or utility knife
- Glitter tape (optional)

Notes / Tips

Try color-matching with this activity by painting different colors around the slots and adding a colored dot to the jar lids.

Play Dough Pinch & Roll Counting Game

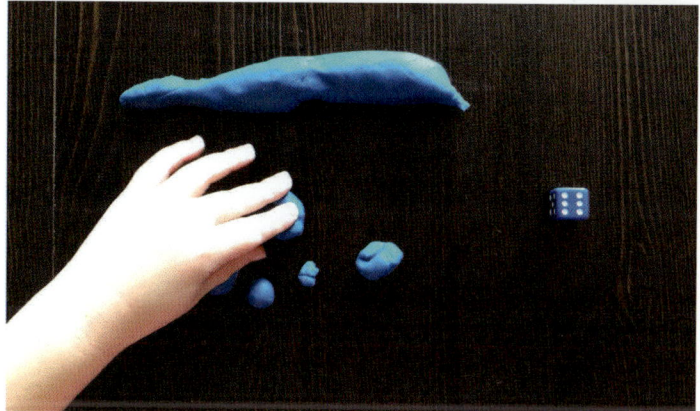
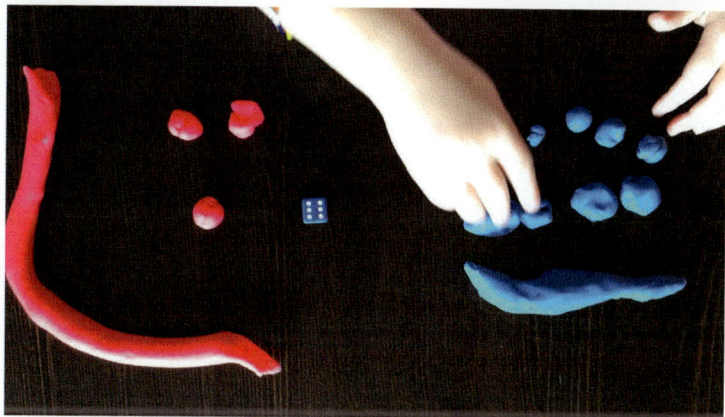

by **Laura Marschel**
Lalymom
Home with two, creativity will brew
www.Lalymom.com

Materials / Supplies

- Play dough for each player
- Die

Notes / Tips

If necessary take a few minutes at the beginning of the game to demonstrate and practice making the play dough into snakes and balls. You can use descriptive words to help your child understand how to hold and manipulate the dough. Flat hands for rolling the snake. You could try two hands together for rolling balls or one hand flat above the table. See which works better for your child.

How to

Give each player an equal portion of play dough. Ideally, each person would have their own color, but it is not essential.

Each player starts by rolling their play dough into a snake shape.

To play the game, each player rolls the game die and pinches off that many finger wide bits of play dough and rolls them into balls. The winner is the first person to roll their entire snake into balls.

Variations:
- Use a ruler to measure each piece to ensure equal sized balls.
- Use a ruler to remove the number of inches or centimeters that are rolled on the game die.
- Use the balls to make shapes, numbers, letters, or your name as you play.
- When you are done, play again in reverse by adding the balls together as you roll the game die.

Early Learning

Object Trace

Materials / Supplies

- Random items such as toys and everyday household objects
- Paper
- Pencil

How to

Lay out a piece of paper. Then place the items on top. Trace around the items with a pencil. Older children may be able to do this for themselves. Once traced, remove the objects, shuffle them around and encourage your child to match them up with the correct outline.

by **Nicolette Roux**
Powerful Mothering
Learning one step at a time
www.PowerfulMothering.com

Notes / Tips

Expand this activity by playing hide and seek with your items after tracing them!

Smashing ABC Moon Rocks

by **Samantha Soper-Caetano**
Stir the Wonder
Inspiring Learning
www.stirthewonder.com

Materials / Supplies

- Flour
- Water
- Gray tempera paint
- Cotton balls
- Baking sheet
- Foil
- Bowl
- Spoon
- Tray
- Toy hammer
- Alphabet flashcards (optional)

How to

This activity is a fun way for toddlers and preschoolers to practice fine motor skills and letter recognition.

First make some "moon rocks" - otherwise known as baked cotton balls. Kids will love helping to make them which is also great for practicing fine motor skills.

Mix up about ½ cup of flour and ½ water in a bowl and add a little squirt of gray tempera paint. Cover a baking sheet with foil. Place a cotton ball in the flour mixture. Coat the cotton ball and then spoon it out onto the baking sheet. Place the baking sheet of cotton balls in a preheated oven and bake for about one hour at 300 degrees Fahrenheit (150 C).

Once the cotton balls are baked, let them cool and use a permanent marker to write some letters on each one. Arrange them on a tray with a toy hammer and invite your child to get smashing!

Use alphabet flashcards and have the children find the matching ABC moon rocks on the tray before smashing it.

Notes / Tips

Some toy hammers may not be strong enough to smash the moon rocks. Try different play tools to work on different fine motor skills.

Early Learning

Art & Crafts

Owl Collage by Georgina, Craftulate

Easy Cut Punch Paste Crafting by Laura, Lalymom

Powdered Chalk Art by Emma, Our Whimsical Days

Yarn Wrapped Music Notes by Dyan, And Next Comes L

Watercolor Drop Painted Bunting by Samantha, Stir the Wonder

Beaded Wind Chime by Emma, Our Whimsical Days

Pom Pom Rainbow by Georgina, Craftulate

Clay Pinch Pots by Kristina, School Time Snippets

Symmetrical Butterfly Straw Painting by Devany, Still Playing School

Yarn Mobiles by Nicolette, Powerful Mothering

Spaghetti Sun by Blayne, House of Burke

Cotton Swab Steam Train Art by Georgina, Craftulate

Stained Glass Art by Nicolette, Powerful Mothering

Seashell Ladybugs by Devany, Still Playing School

Owl Collage

by **Georgina Bomer**
Craftulate
Making. Learning. Fun.
www.craftulate.com

How to

Print the outline onto white cardstock. Provide your child with the scrap paper and let them get to work punching out circles. Using the paper punch is great for strengthening hand muscles.

Once they have punched out a good amount of circles, show them how to glue the paper onto the template. Manipulating those little bits of paper really works on the pincer grasp! Keep punching and gluing until the owl is complete.

Your child could also go one step further and add some white circles for the eyes too.

Materials / Supplies

- Owl outline - You can find these by searching online or you could draw one freehand!
- Card
- Scrap paper with a variety of patterns and colors
- Circle paper punches
- Glue

Notes / Tips

Use two different color tones of paper, one for the owl's body and one for the owl's wings.

Easy Cut Punch Paste Crafting

by **Laura Marschel**
Lalymom
Home with two, creativity will brew
www.Lalymom.com

Materials / Supplies

- Construction paper
- Assorted paper punches
- Glue stick or glue
- Safety scissors

How to

Lay out the materials on your desk or table and show your child how to work the various paper punches. Be sure to show that it makes a shape cut out as well as a hole in the paper. Both can be fun to craft with!

Together you can make anything your imagination dreams up by cutting, punching and pasting shapes together. Here are some ideas to try:

- Hearts to create Valentines
- Stars, stripes, and fireworks shapes for 4th of July or creating flags
- Decorate Easter egg cut outs
- Punch red circles and paste them on an apple tree
- Punch black shapes and decorate a pumpkin
- Punch all colors and decorate a Christmas Tree
- Use black or gray paper as a background for making robots
- Use large circle punches to make wheels for vehicles
- Make faces
- Design some food like cupcakes, veggies, or ice cream
- Add googly eyes or use circle punches to create funny monsters
- Cut out letters of the alphabet and use the punches to trace them

Notes / Tips

You could draw some guidelines for cutting. Try straight lines, zigzags, and wavy lines. See what creations your child can create with the various cut outs and paper punches.

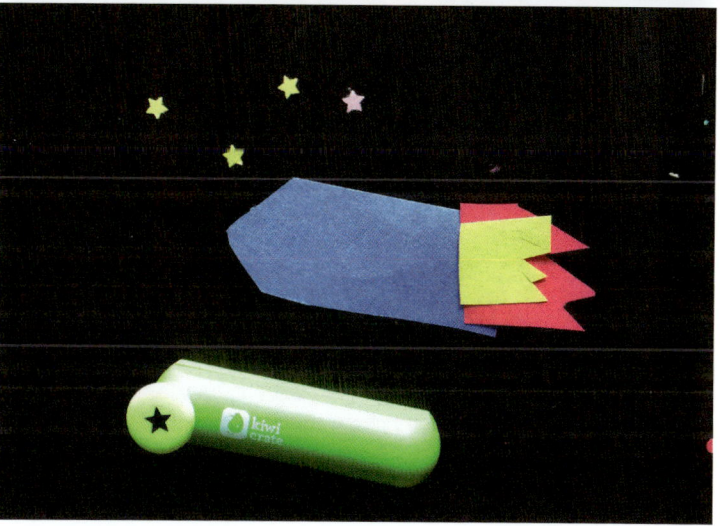

Art & Crafts

Powdered Chalk Art

How to

This activity is more of a process art kind of project than a keep-it-for-always work of art, but it is fun and great for fine motor skills!

The only advance preparation required is grating the chalk, which is a job for an adult. This step can take a while and can be quite messy, so I recommend doing it outside.

Set out the rest of the materials and invite your child to get creative.

Demonstrate how to take a pinch of the chalk and sprinkle it onto the paper. If your child does not want to touch the chalk, then a spoon can be used to scatter it on the paper instead.

Then comes the fun part - spray bottle time! To add a science element, ask questions such as, "How does it change?" When the art dries, it will be back to dry chalk again.

by **Emma Craig**
Our Whimsical Days
Memories in the making
www.ourwhimsicaldays.com

Materials / Supplies

- Cheese grater
- Heavy paper (we often use the inside of cereal boxes)
- Spray bottle
- Sidewalk chalk

Notes / Tips

My daughter loves to use this grated chalk as "fairy dust." More of that pinching and sprinkling it all over the yard is working her fine motor and imagination muscles - and it all rinses away in the next rain!

Yarn Wrapped Music Notes

How to

This craft works best for older children as younger children may find the wrapping process tricky. My five year old could do the craft independently, but occasionally struggled to pull the yarn tight enough. My three year old, on the other hand, needed help with this craft so I provided hand-over-hand assistance to help him get started.

To prepare this activity, cut some cardboard into music note shapes. Then cut slits around the entire edge of the music notes. These slits are what holds the yarn in place as the kids wrap the cardboard. Wrap the cardboard with yarn until the cardboard is well covered. When the cardboard is fully covered, cut the yarn and tuck it behind some of the wrapped yarn and into a slit to secure it into place.

by **Dyan Robson**
And Next Comes L
Hyperlexia + Autism + Other Tales of Learning
www.andnextcomesL.com

Materials / Supplies

- Cardboard
- Scissors
- Black yarn

Notes / Tips

Turn these yarn wrapped music notes into a mobile by hanging them from the ceiling.

Watercolor Drop Painted Bunting

How to

From squeezing pipettes for watercolor painting to cutting and threading, this colorful craft will give kids lots of fine motor exercise! Plus, they will have a beautiful decoration to show for all their hard work!

Paint the paper towels with liquid watercolors using the drip painting method with pipettes or droppers. Use a tray or cookie sheet while drip painting to catch the excess paint so it does not get all over the place.

Set the painted paper towels aside to dry. Depending on how wet they are, it may take awhile for them to dry completely. Lay the wet paper towels to dry on craft paper or newspaper for quick and easy clean up.

When the painted paper towels are dry, you or your child(ren) can cut out the triangles for the bunting. Then you or your kids can punch holes in the tops of the triangles to prepare them for threading. Using a hole punch is great way for kids to practice fine motor skills too!

When all the triangles are cut and hole punched, they are ready for threading. Simply thread some yarn through a plastic yarn needle so kids can easily string up the triangle bunting.

Tie some loops at the ends of the yarn and the bunting is ready to be hung up in a bright window!

by **Samantha Soper-Caetano**
Stir the Wonder
Inspiring Learning
www.stirthewonder.com

Materials / Supplies

- Liquid watercolor paint
- Pipettes or droppers
- Paper towels
- Scissors
- Hole punch
- Yarn
- Plastic yarn needles
- Craft tray

Notes / Tips

Use cookie cutters as a stencil to create a garland with different shapes to fit any season or theme.

Beaded Wind Chime

by **Emma Craig**
Our Whimsical Days
Memories in the making
www.ourwhimsicaldays.com

Materials / Supplies

- Old keys
- Acrylic paint
- 2 wooden dowels
- Jingle bells
- Beads
- Pipe cleaner
- Ribbon or string

How to

The first task is to paint the keys. They may need a few coats of acrylic paint to really get covered. While they dry, invite your child to start stringing the beads onto the ribbon, adding in bells once or twice to each ribbon.

Next, attach the two dowels together to form an X-shape using a pipe cleaner.

Add the finished keys to the end of the beaded ribbons and tie them to the dowels, making sure they are just close enough so they made a delightful "clinking" sound when they tap together.

To hang it up, add another ribbon to each of the dowel ends, gather them into a bunch and tie them in a knot.

Notes / Tips

If your child likes to make patterns, then the beads are a perfect material to explore with.

[Printable]

Pom Pom Rainbow

by **Georgina Bomer**
Craftulate
Making. Learning. Fun.
www.craftulate.com

Materials / Supplies

- Rainbow Template free printable
- White card
- Contact paper
- Scissors
- Tape
- Small pom poms in rainbow colors

How to

Print out the free rainbow template onto white cardstock. Note: The rainbow image has been simplified to only six colors so that it corresponds with popular colors of pom poms that are widely available.

Cut a piece of contact paper so that it is slightly larger than the cardstock, remove the backing paper and place it (sticky side up) over the rainbow. Then tape the edges of the contact paper to the work surface, so the rainbow is stuck underneath.

Provide your child with a container of pom poms and let them create a rainbow picture by matching up the colors.

This activity works on pincer grasp (as those small pom poms can be fiddly!), but also hand-eye coordination to get the pom pom into the correct position. And, of course, it is great for color recognition too!

Once the rainbow is complete, you can remove all the pom poms so that another child can try the activity, or so your child can start again!

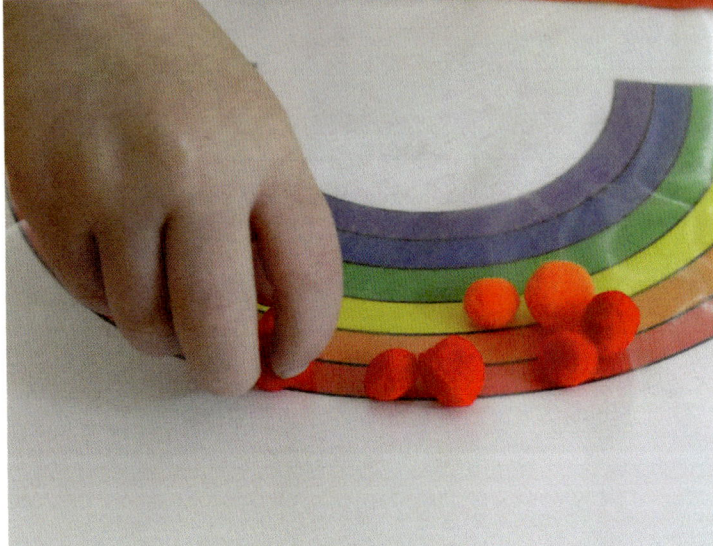

Notes / Tips

This technique could be used for all kinds of pictures – anything that you think your child would enjoy!

Clay Pinch Pots

by **Kristina Couturier**
School Time Snippets
Learn and play today
www.schooltimesnippets.com

Notes / Tips

These clay bowls make a great homemade gift to give to special family members!

Materials / Supplies

- Air dry clay
- Wax paper
- Paint (optional)

How to

Set out a sheet of wax paper or a work tray. Grab a handful of air dry clay and have your child roll it into a ball. Keep in mind that the more clay they use, the bigger and/or thicker the finished product.

Invite your child to stick a thumb into the clay to make an opening. Then encourage your child to pinch away at the sides to form a bowl. Continue pinching until satisfied with the shape of the bowl.

Let the clay bowl dry for a day or two. If they like, the kids could always paint the bowls to add some color!

Art & Crafts

Symmetrical Butterfly Straw Painting

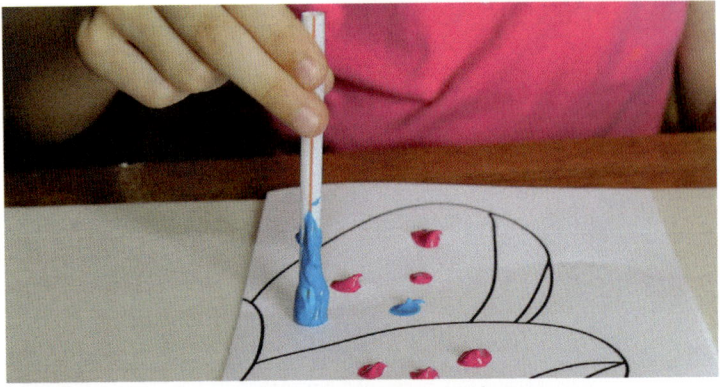
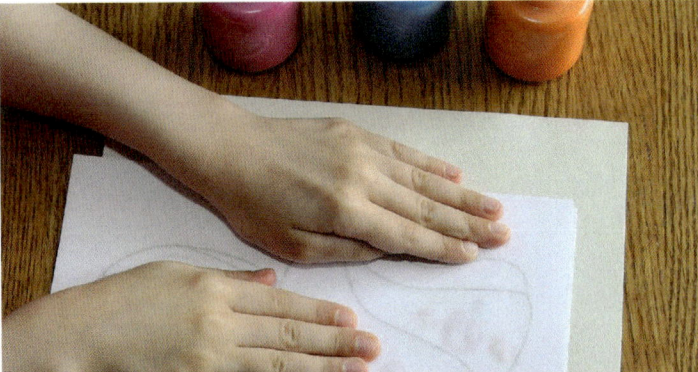

How to

This bright and cheerful craft for kids uses several fine motor skills to create a symmetrical butterfly painting. We loved the result so much that we had to make several!

Have children fold the printed butterfly coloring sheets in half right down the center creating two symmetrical sides. Help the kids carefully fold the sheets again in the opposite direction so you will only be painting on half of the butterfly's body.

Ask children to cut the straws. Dip the trimmed straws in the paint. This technique is the perfect way to distribute just enough paint on the paper while simultaneously working on fine motor skills. Keep reminding the kids, "Dip, dot, dip, dot," as they are painting!

Once the painting is complete, carefully fold the page back the other way again. Show children how to press and smooth the paper to spread the paint around the butterfly's wings without any mess.

When you open the paper, you will have a perfectly symmetrical painting! Once the paint dries, invite children to cut out their butterflies.

by **Devany LeDrew**
Still Playing School
Playing, learning, remembering
www.stillplayingschool.com

Materials / Supplies

- Butterfly coloring sheets or drawings
- Straws
- Scissors
- Paint

Notes / Tips

These butterflies look great hanging up as a display. The wings flow out in a 3D way since the paper has been folded.

{100} 100 Fine Motor Ideas

Yarn Mobiles

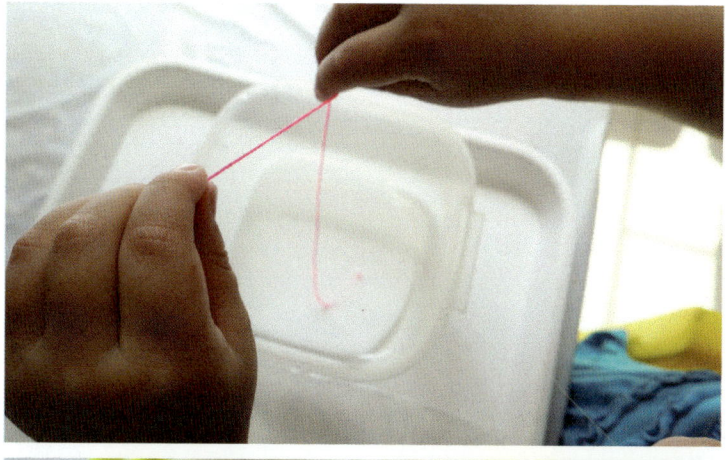
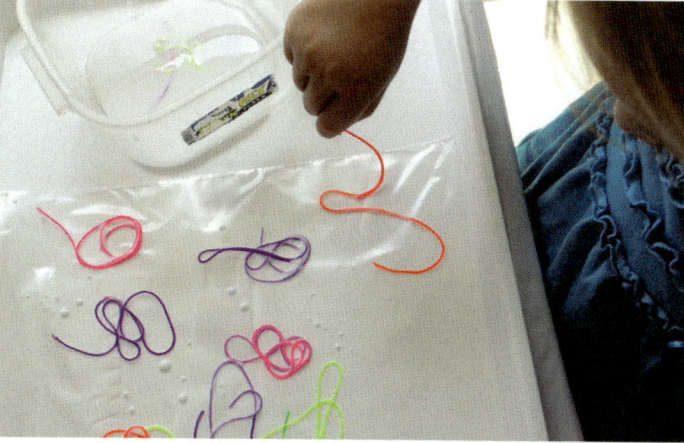
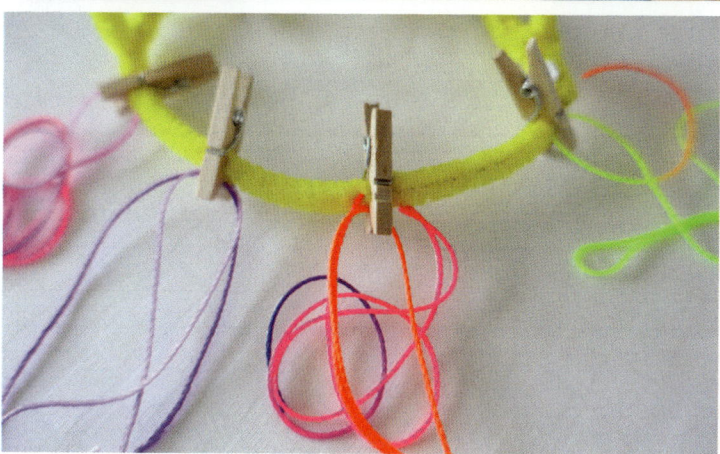

by **Nicolette Roux**
Powerful Mothering
Learning one step at a time
www.PowerfulMothering.com

Materials / Supplies

- Yarn or string
- White school glue
- Plastic such as a zipper seal bag
- Tray
- Bowl
- 3 pipe cleaners
- 8-10 mini clothespins

Notes / Tips

Using a tray for your activities allows you to easily move the activity to other areas to dry.

How to

This activity is split into two sessions. First, you will need to make the yarn ornaments.

Cut strips of yarn or string the length of your forearm, about eight-ten pieces. Mix the glue with a bit of water in the bowl to make it runnier. Lay out your bag in the tray and put the bowl of glue next to it. Show your child how to take a bit of yarn and completely submerge it in the watered down glue. Then pick it up (letting it drip off a bit) and place it on the plastic of the closed zipper seal bag in a squiggly and overlapping manner. Encourage your child to complete the other bits of yarn. Leave it to dry.

Once dry, carefully peel the yarn off the plastic. See how nice it formed?

Next, make a circle with two pipe cleaners using the third pipe cleaner to make a hanging hook. Encourage your child to attach the yarn with the mini clothespins to the pipe cleaners!

Hang it up somewhere to enjoy!

Spaghetti Sun

by **Blayne Burke**
House of Burke
Learning and exploring together as a family!
www.houseofburkeblog.com

How to

This spaghetti sun is a multi-faceted craft project with several components. To start, give your child a paper plate and some yellow washable paint. Invite them to cover the entire plate with the paint. Once that is dry, encourage them to squeeze glue onto each one of the indentations on the paper plate. This is a serious fine motor workout, even for adults! Gripping and squeezing helps build and develop muscles in the fingers.

Once the glue is applied to the indentations on the plate, have your little one take pieces of pot-ready spaghetti and gently lay them on the strips of glue. Cover the entire plate with the pasta and let it dry. Once dry, the sun looks fantastic up on the window!

Materials / Supplies

- Pot-ready spaghetti
- Paper plate
- Yellow washable paint
- Paintbrush
- Glue

Notes / Tips

This activity would be fantastic paired with a weather unit.

Cotton Swab Steam Train Art

Printable

by **Georgina Bomer**
Craftulate
Making. Learning. Fun.
www.craftulate.com

Materials / Supplies

- Cotton Swab Train Free Printable
- Cotton Swabs
- Paint

Notes / Tips

Use painters' tape to secure the paper to your work surface or table. This tip is particularly useful for younger children!

How to

Print out your free blank train template and get all your materials ready. If you can find those tiny pots of paint (in the kid's paint section of craft stores), then these are perfect for cotton swabs!

Show your child how to dip the end of the cotton swab in the paint and dab it into the circles on the train picture.

It takes quite a bit of time to complete this picture, so younger children may not have the patience to see it through to the end. Remember that it does not have to be completed all in one session!

As well as producing a really pretty picture, this activity is great for working on your child's fine motor skills by holding the cotton swab and then manipulating it so that the paint goes exactly in the circle on template.

Art & Crafts {103}

Stained Glass Art

by **Nicolette Roux**
Powerful Mothering
Learning one step at a time
www.PowerfulMothering.com

Materials / Supplies

- Large sheets of paper or cardstock
- Large tray
- Cardboard tubes
- Black paint
- Watercolors

How to

Place the paper in a tray to make it easier to pick up, move, and stack (by rotating) to dry. Alternatively you can just tape the paper to the table.

Put some black paint in a dish and let the kids get stamping with the cardboard tubes making overlapping circles. Showing your child the images of this tutorial will help them understand overlapping better.

Once their paper is full of circles, leave it to dry. We stamped in the morning and painted in the afternoon.

Once dry, use the watercolor paints to paint each little section of the circles with a different color.

Notes / Tips

It is ART! If your child has trouble completing the steps, then do not be discouraged. Your child is having fun and still doing something fine motor even if the end result is not what we, as adults, would desire. Try again in a few months!

Seashell Ladybugs

by **Devany LeDrew**
Still Playing School
Playing, learning, remembering
www.stillplayingschool.com

Materials / Supplies

- Seashells
- Liquid watercolor paints
- Eyedroppers
- Markers

How to

Use the eyedropper to slowly drop the liquid watercolors on to the shells. The porous surface of the shells will absorb the paint beautifully. You can even try blending colors for pretty results!

Allow the shells to dry. We left ours outside in the sun to dry.

Add the details of the lady bugs with markers. Draw on a head, divide the body, and add spots.

Notes / Tips

These colorful ladybugs are the perfect loose parts for play and learning! Sort by color, size, and count and add the spots, etc.

{106}

Seasonal Holidays

Cake Decorating Craft by Kristina, School Time Snippets

Groundhog Finger Puppet by Devany, Still Playing School

Valentine's Day Loom Band Hearts by Laura, Lalymom

Painting Rainbows with Combs by Blayne, House of Burke

Easter Garland by Laura, Lalymom

Easter Egg Match by Georgina, Craftulate

Apple Color Sorting Tray by Dyan, And Next Comes L

Pumpkin Patch by Blayne, House of Burke

Spooky Spider Web by Sarah, Little Bins For Little Hands

Clothespin Feathers Turkey by Samantha, Stir the Wonder

Candy Cane Garland by Georgina, Craftulate

Gumdrop Structures by Sarah, Little Bins For Little Hands

Paper Plate Christmas Wreath by Kristina, School Time Snippets

Baked Cotton Ball Snowman by Devany, Still Playing School

Cake Decorating Craft

How to

Learn the art of cake decorating with this fun fine motor skills craft!

First, find and print a birthday cake coloring page online.

Invite your child to choose different colors of puffy paint to outline and decorate the birthday cake by squeezing the paint onto the paper.

Continue squeezing the paint until your child is happy with the design.

Once the paint has dried, turn it into a birthday card!

by **Kristina Couturier**
School Time Snippets -
Learn and play today
www.schooltimesnippets.com

Materials / Supplies

- Birthday cake printable
- Fabric puffy paint (found in the fabric aisle at the craft store)

Notes / Tips

For a fun twist, squeeze the paint onto wax paper. The finished product can be attached to the window as window clings!

Groundhog Finger Puppet

by **Devany LeDrew**
Still Playing School
Playing, learning, remembering
www.stillplayingschool.com

Materials / Supplies

- Egg carton
- Green paint
- Brown pom pom
- Smaller pink or black pom pom (for the nose)
- Googly eyes
- Brown construction paper
- Glue

How to

Do you know the tradition of Groundhog Day? The groundhog emerges from his den on February 2nd. If he sees his shadow, then he returns to his burrow for six more weeks of winter. If he does not see his shadow, then it means that spring will arrive early.

Invite your child to paint one section of an egg carton green. An adult should carefully cut a hole in the top to make the groundhog's burrow.

Craft your groundhog using pom poms for the body and nose! Glue on googly eyes and construction paper for tiny groundhog ears.

Place the pom pom groundhog so that he's peeking out of the top of his egg carton burrow. The puppet becomes a fun fine motor activity as he peeks in and out of his home to look for his shadow!

Notes / Tips

We live in the state of Pennsylvania, which is also home to the famous groundhog Punxsutawney Phil!

Seasonal Holidays

Valentine's Day Loom Band Hearts

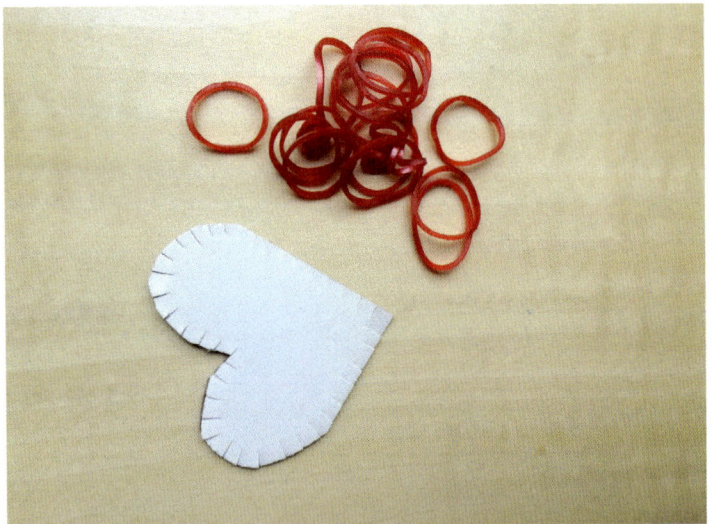

by **Laura Marschel**
Lalymom
Home with two, creativity will brew
www.Lalymom.com

Materials / Supplies

- Red loom bands
- Corrugated cardboard (white if possible)
- Strong scissors or kitchen shears

How to

Cut out a few hearts from the corrugated cardboard, roughly two inches by two inches, making the right angle of the cardboard into the bottom point of the heart. Snip tiny cuts all the way around the heart for the loom bands to catch on to.

Place the hearts and loom bands into your busy bag and you are all set. You may or may not choose to place a loom band or two onto one of the hearts to show what to do.

This simple activity takes advantage of the pretty colors the loom bands come in and makes it a preschooler-friendly activity! Of course be careful of setting out loom bands if you have babies or toddlers who still put things into their mouths.

I recommend using corrugated cardboard simply because paper, cardstock, or even single-layer cardboard are too flimsy and would buckle under the pressure of the elastic loom bands. When you are picking out cardboard for this activity, please stick to the thick stuff!

Notes / Tips

Cut out the heart and draw the lines for the cuts all the way around and ask your older child to do the snips.

Painting Rainbows with Combs

by **Blayne Burke**
House of Burke
Learning and exploring together as a family!
www.houseofburkeblog.com

Materials / Supplies

- Washable paint
- Comb
- Cardstock
- Paper plate

Notes / Tips

Try painting with different sized combs or a brush. Compare the different sizes of the rainbows and the different textures!

How to

We love celebrating St. Patrick's Day over here! We also love using unconventional materials to paint with. This simple and fun activity is a fantastic way to learn about colors while making a festive decoration for the holiday. What says St. Patrick's Day more than rainbows? We love exploring the nature and colors of rainbows!

To set up your rainbow craft project, get a paper plate and squeeze washable paint in the colors of the rainbow: red, orange, yellow, green, blue, purple. In this activity, your child will be using a fine tooth comb to comb out the colors. Provide one next to the paint on the paper plate. Set out a piece of cardstock, and encourage your child to dip the comb in the paint and brush it onto the paper. Make sure that they pick up each of the paint colors on the bristles of the comb.

Encourage them to sweep the comb in different directions. Practice making arches like true rainbows or let them paint freely. Have your child identify all of the colors of the rainbow as they paint.

Easter Garland

How to

Print out your Design-an-Egg Printable (if you are using it) and allow the ink to dry.

For the DIY Version, mark the height of your cookie cutter three times on the construction paper and then using a straight edge, make lines across the paper at each mark to make three strips of paper. Trace your cookie cutter once on each strip, all the way to the left side.

Continue as follows for both versions.

Allow your child to cut on all the straight lines. Next fold the strips of paper like an accordion starting on the right edge of the shapes. When they are all folded, cut the eggs out, making sure not to cut the edge of the paper where you want the eggs to stay connected. Unfold and you are ready to color them in! Once you are done, you can tape them together to make one long garland.

by **Laura Marschel**
Lalymom
Home with two, creativity will brew
www.Lalymom.com

Materials / Supplies

- Safety scissors
- Crayons or markers
- Tape
- Cookie cutters (for DIY version)
- Straight edge (for DIY version)
- Easter egg garland printable (for Printable version)

Notes / Tips

If the thickness of the paper makes it too hard you can do the cutting and leave the tracing and coloring steps to your child. You could also make it using tissue paper to make the cutting easier.

Easter Egg Match

by **Georgina Bomer**
Craftulate
Making. Learning. Fun.
www.craftulate.com

Materials / Supplies

- Plastic Easter eggs, broken in half
- White card or paper
- Pencils, pens, crayons
- Container

Notes / Tips

This activity would be great for an older sibling to prepare for a younger one.

How to

Draw several Easter egg outlines onto the card and draw a line across the middle to show the two different halves. Then color each half differently to match the eggs.

Either keep all the egg outlines together on one sheet or cut them into individual cards.

Then place everything into the container (I reused an Easter basket from the previous year) and present it to your child.

Depending on their age and ability, you may need to demonstrate how the eggs fit together and that the top and bottom halves are different.

Once they understand the concept, they will find that those eggs can be quite fiddly to close together, which is great fine motor practice!

If they get the hang of the game and want to keep playing, then try timing them to see how fast they can match up all of the eggs.

Seasonal Holidays {113}

Apple Color Sorting Tray

by **Dyan Robson**
And Next Comes L
Hyperlexia + Autism + Other Tales of Learning
www.andnextcomesL.com

Materials / Supplies

- Acrylic apples
- Tongs
- Tray with two sides or small cups or bowls
- Paper
- Marker or pen

How to

On two pieces of paper, write the words "red" and "green." For kids who cannot read yet, you can write the words in the corresponding color or draw a blob of color instead. Set out the apples in front of the tray and label each compartment of the tray with the labelled pieces of paper.

Using the tongs, have the kids pick up and transfer the apples to the correct spot in the tray. We love to use these yellow squeezer tweezers since they are extremely easy for little hands to operate. Tongs from the kitchen would work just as well. Simply scoop up one apple at a time and move it to the correct spot.

If you cannot find acrylic apples, then try this activity using colored glass stones or buttons instead.

Notes / Tips

Instead of writing color words, write numbers and have the kids transfer and count the correct number of apples.

{114} 100 Fine Motor Ideas

Pumpkin Patch

by **Blayne Burke**
House of Burke
Learning and exploring together as a family!
www.houseofburkeblog.com

Materials / Supplies

- Shoebox
- Brown construction paper
- Green marker
- Acrylic pumpkins
- Plastic tweezers
- Tape or glue
- Scissors
- Cup

How to

This fine motor pumpkin patch is such a creative way to recreate pumpkin picking on a smaller scale!

To create your pumpkin patch, cover a shoe box in brown construction paper. You want to make sure that you can still get into the box. On the top of the box, cut 16 holes right through the paper and cardboard using your scissors. Once your holes are cut, use your green marker to draw decorative vines around the holes. Set out a cup full of acrylic pumpkins and a pair of plastic tweezers.

Encourage your little one to use the tweezers to pick up the pumpkins and drop them into the holes in the patch. Once your child puts all of the pumpkins into the patch, they can use the tweezers to pluck them back out! This activity utilizes both fine motor skills and hand-eye coordination.

Notes / Tips

You could easily turn your pumpkin patch into a math activity. Have your young toddler count the pumpkins as the put them into the patch or pick them out. Older kiddos can learn simple addition or subtraction by picking a certain amount of pumpkins out and putting a certain amount back in. Be creative!

Seasonal Holidays

Spooky Spider Web

by **Sarah McClelland**
Little Bins For Little Hands
A Sensory Filled Life
www.littlebinsforlittlehands.com

Materials / Supplies

- Fake spider web decoration
- Plastic spiders
- Scissors (optional)

How to

This activity is quick and easy to set up and is perfect for Halloween! Take a large pile of fake spider web material and add a variety of plastic spiders to it. Make sure that the spiders really get stuck to the web!

Your kids' task is to remove the spiders. It's tricky! Your kids will have to work on their finger dexterity skills to manipulate the spider web to remove the spiders.

This is a perfect fine motor activity for a variety of ages. Young kids can simply use their fingers to remove the spiders. Or add a pair of scissors for older kids to cut the spiders free. Several ages can enjoy this activity together. Even pulling the webbing apart is great for hand strength. Have your kids wrap the webbing around the spiders or have your kids hide the spiders for other kids to find.

Notes / Tips

When finished, put the web and spiders in a sealable bag and save it as a quiet time busy bag!

Clothespin Feathers Turkey

by **Samantha Soper-Caetano**
Stir the Wonder
Inspiring Learning
www.stirthewonder.com

Materials / Supplies

- Brown craft foam
- Triangle shaped foam sticker
- Teardrop shaped foam sticker
- 6-8 clothespins
- Variety of colorful feathers
- Googly eyes
- Hot glue gun

Notes / Tips

Do not worry about where your child places the feathers on the turkey. What matters is that they are working on their skills.

How to

To make a clothespin feathers turkey, cut one bigger circle and one smaller circle out of brown craft foam. Hot glue the two circles together.

Add a turkey face using googly eyes and foam sticker shapes for the beak and wattle (the flappy red part on a turkey's neck).

For the feather clothespins, hot glue small craft feathers onto standard wooden clothespins.

Children of all ages will enjoy clipping the clothespin feathers on and off while working on hand strengthening and practicing fine motor skills. You can also use this activity as an opportunity to teach or review colors with your kids.

Candy Cane Garland

How to

Prepare the activity in advance by cutting the pipe cleaners in half using wire cutters. This job is for an adult.

Show your child how to twist one red and one white pipe cleaner together to make the candy cane stripes. If this twisting is too difficult, then you can provide hand-over-hand assistance or they can just use plain red and white ones.

Next, show them how to create a pipe cleaner ring then link the next pipe cleaner to it. This part really works those little hands and it takes a lot of coordination to twist the ends together to make a ring.

Keep going until a long garland has been formed. Then use it for some seasonal decoration!

by **Georgina Bomer**
Craftulate
Making. Learning. Fun.
www.craftulate.com

Materials / Supplies

- Red pipe cleaners
- White pipe cleaners
- Wire cutters

Notes / Tips

Note: Be aware that the wire at each end of the pipe cleaners can be sharp. Fold over the ends if you are concerned.

Gumdrop Structures

by **Sarah McClelland**
Little Bins For Little Hands
A Sensory Filled Life
www.littlebinsforlittlehands.com

Materials / Supplies

- Gumdrops
- Toothpicks

How to

This gumdrop structure building activity is super simple to set up and perfect for fine motor skills practice. Building with gumdrops will keep the kids busy when you are baking, or if you are stuck inside on a cold day! If you have made a holiday gingerbread house, then you will probably have quite a few gumdrops on hand.

Set out a container of gumdrops and a bowl of toothpicks (or dump the toothpicks on the table like my son did!). Now for the fun part! Start building your gumdrop structure. What will you make?

Several different grasps can be worked on all at once including the pincer grasp (thumb and first finger) while pushing in the toothpick and the tripod grasp (thumb and first two fingers) for holding the gumdrops. Both of these grasps are important for handwriting later on. Gumdrops come in different sizes. The larger ones will be easier to start with if necessary.

Notes / Tips

Parents can also enjoy building. Make a structure and see if your child can copy it for both visual skills and fine motor work!

Paper Plate Christmas Wreath

How to

Practice those scissor skills with this seasonal paper plate wreath!

First, prepare the activity by cutting a circle from the middle of the paper plate.

Show your child how to snip at the paper plate with scissors to make a "fringe." Encourage your child to snip all around the paper plate. When your child is finished, punch two holes in the paper plate and add the ribbon.

Next, give your child sticker gems or another kind of embellishment to place around the paper plate.

Add a bit of mess to this project by using white paper plates and paint them green or by using mini pom poms and/or sequins and glue instead of the gem stickers.

by **Kristina Couturier**
School Time Snippets
Learn and play today
www.schooltimesnippets.com

Materials / Supplies

- Paper plate
- Gem stickers
- Scissors
- Ribbon
- Hole punch

Notes / Tips

Make a wreath for any occasion. Buy different colored plates and embellishments to make spring, summer, fall, winter, sport season, or birthday wreaths!

Baked Cotton Ball Snowman

Materials / Supplies

- Cotton balls
- Flour
- Water
- Baking sheet
- Oven
- Googly eyes
- Markers
- Toothpicks

by **Devany LeDrew**
Still Playing School
Playing, learning, remembering
www.stillplayingschool.com

How to

Baked cotton ball snowmen are the perfect fine motor winter craft!

Ask your child to mix together equal parts flour and water until you have a thick paste. Dip the cotton balls into the mixture until they are completely covered. This part is messy, but fun!

Put the coated cotton balls onto a baking sheet. You can stack three cotton balls vertically or horizontally to create snowmen bodies or you can bake them individually. We loved all three options! Bake the cotton balls at 300 degrees F for 30 to 40 minutes. They will harden as they cook.

Once baked and cooled, you can glue individual baked cotton balls together to make snowmen or decorate the ones you pre-assembled before baking.

Glue on googly eyes, add details with markers, and gently stick toothpicks in for arms. I poked holes in the baked cotton balls first with scissors and then let our kids stick the toothpicks into the holes. Use a marker to color the tip of a toothpick orange and break it off if you want a "carrot" nose. Adults should supervise the breaking and poking of toothpicks and, as always, use your best judgement about the safety and abilities of your children.

Notes / Tips

The snowmen can be made into fridge magnets or used in small world play!

Fine Motor Merchandise on Zazzle

Shirts, Mugs, Totes, Posters, and More!

www.zazzle.com/finemotor

More Resources for Fine Motor Skills

Visit us on our blogs for tons more fine motor activities! We share something every Friday!

Blayne Burke at **House of Burke**
Learning and exploring together as a family!
www.houseofburkeblog.com

Dyan Robson at **And Next Comes L**
Hyperlexia + Autism + Other Tales of Learning
www.andnextcomesL.com

Kristina Couturier at **School Time Snippets**
Learn and play today
www.schooltimesnippets.com

Devany LeDrew at **Still Playing School**
Playing, learning, remembering
www.stillplayingschool.com

Laura Marschel at **Lalymom**
Home with two, creativity will brew
www.Lalymom.com

Georgina Bomer at **Craftulate**
Making. Learning. Fun.
www.craftulate.com

Nicolette Roux at **Powerful Mothering**
Learning one step at a time
www.PowerfulMothering.com

by Emma Craig at **Our Whimsical Days**
Memories in the making
www.ourwhimsicaldays.com

Sarah McClelland at **Little Bins For Little Hands**
A Sensory Filled Life
www.littlebinsforlittlehands.com

Samantha Soper-Caetano at **Stir the Wonder**
Inspiring Learning
www.stirthewonder.com

100 Fine Motor Ideas for Parents, Teachers & Therapists
Toys - Busy Bags - Sensory - Practical Life - Early Learning - Art & Crafts - Seasonal & Holiday

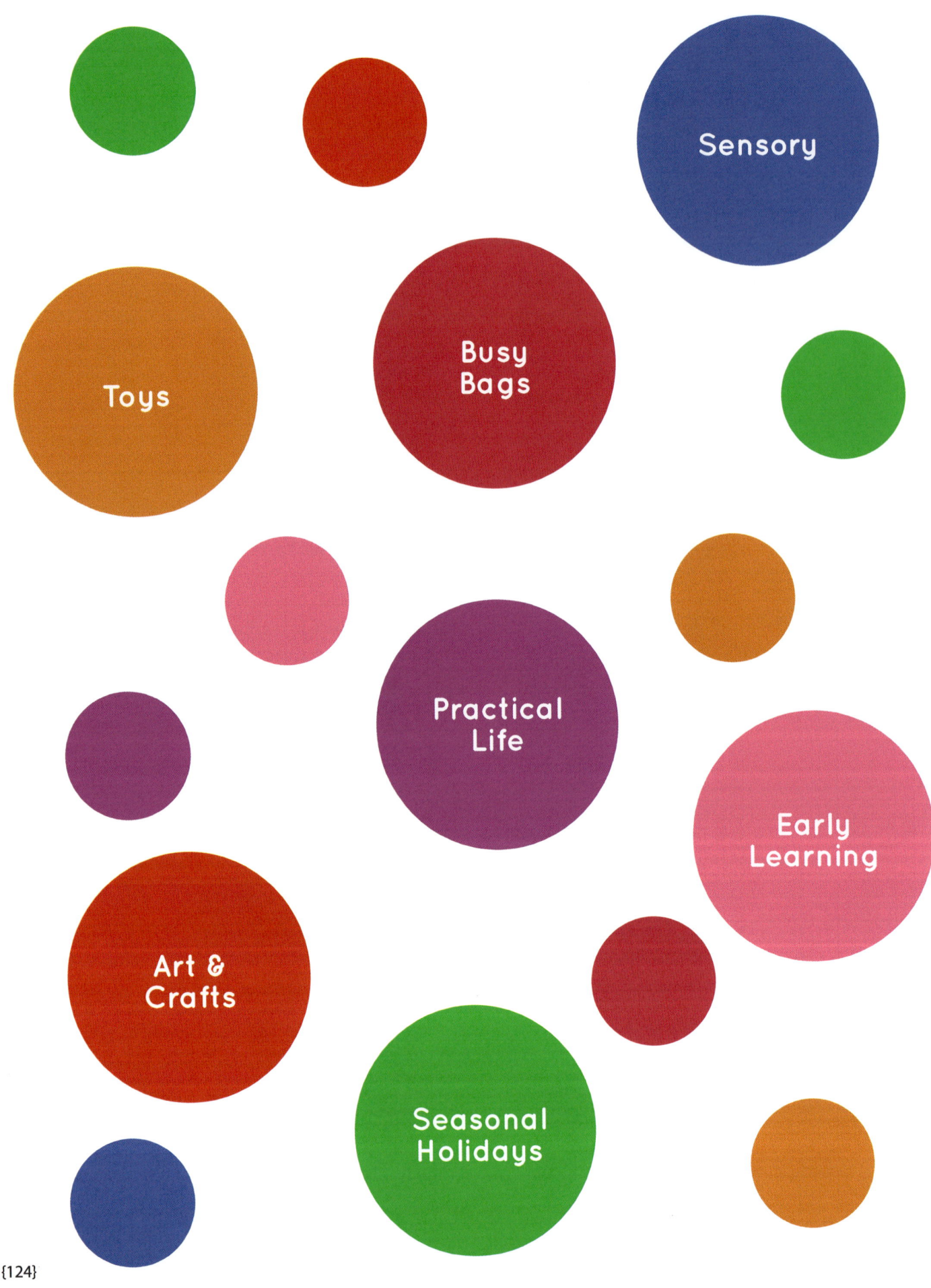

Index

100 Fine Motor Ideas for Parents, Teachers & Therapists

Toys - Busy Bags - Sensory - Practical Life - Early Learning - Art & Crafts - Seasonal & Holiday

A
air dry clay 99
aliens 30
alphabet 31, 37, 45, 47, 50, 53, 75, 77, 78, 79, 82, 87, 89, 93
aluminum foil 34, 60
And Next Comes L 5, 11, 29, 45, 46, 53, 62, 75, 76, 95, 114
animals 11, 13, 55, 69
ants, plastic 80
apples 93, 114
Art 91-105

B
baking soda 83
balloons 44
basketball 82
beach 56
beads 24, 36, 37, 38, 51, 52, 79, 97,
beans 48
bike washing 65
birds 14, 92
birthday card 108
blocks 17, 51, 81
body parts 41
bracelets 33, 79
brushing 69, 71
bubble wrap 39
building 10, 11, 18, 23, 37, 85, 119
bull's eye 15
bunting 96
Busy Bags 27-41
busy box 86
butterflies 100
buttons 35, 46, 48, 51, 55, 57, 76, 114

C
cake decorating 108
candy cane 118
car track 22
cardboard tube 68, 104
chains 31, 33
chalk 94
Christmas 33, 83, 93, 118, 119, 120
citrus 45
clay 99
clothes washing 61
clothespins 11, 30, 40, 41, 61, 77, 101
cocktail stirrers 53
collage 92
color mixing 22
color sorting 17, 28, 31, 35, 53, 64, 85, 86
combs 111

construction see building
contact paper 32, 74, 98
cookie cutters 78, 83, 112
cotton balls 89, 121
cotton swabs 103
counting see numbers
craft foam 11, 16, 28, 30, 31, 78, 117
craft sticks 40
Crafts 91-105
Craftulate 4, 10, 28, 44, 60, 74, 92, 98, 103, 113, 118
cream, whipped 57
crumpling 15, 82
cups 22, 35, 46, 54, 56
cutting 17, 60, 68, 70

D
dice 48, 80, 81, 87
dinosaurs 13, 19
drawing 45, 50, 56, 71, 76
drawstring bag 67

E
Early Learning 73-89
Easter 74, 93, 112, 113
egg carton 109
eggs, plastic 113
essential oils 45, 46, 64
experiments 83
eye droppers 83, 96, 105

F
fabric puffy paint 108
fairies 19
feathers 14, 24, 46, 117
finger isolation 47
finger strength 28, 31, 40, 44, 85, 102
fish 78
flashlight 62
flowers 19, 74
foil, aluminum 34, 60
folding 63, 66, 100
food preparation 60

G
garland 33, 112, 118
gifts 66, 99
gluing 32, 76, 92, 93, 102, 109, 121
googly eyes 30, 37, 47, 52, 68, 93, 109, 117, 121
groundhogs 109
gumdrops 119

Index

100 Fine Motor Ideas for Parents, Teachers & Therapists
Toys - Busy Bags - Sensory - Practical Life - Early Learning - Art & Crafts - Seasonal & Holiday

H
hair gel 47
hand strengthening 15, 18, 29, 31, 37, 38, 44, 64, 74, 78, 92, 116, 117
hand-eye coordination 10, 14, 18, 25, 28, 30, 37, 47, 53, 64, 66, 74, 80, 85, 98, 115
hearts 74, 93, 110
Holidays 107-121
hose 65
House of Burke 4, 13, 14, 25, 34, 41, 54, 66, 102, 111, 115
hunting 52, 57, 62

I
ice cube tray 48, 80

J
jar lids 60, 83, 86
jingle bells 97

K
keys 62, 97
kinetic sand 54
kitchen science 83
knife skills 17, 60, 70

L
lacing 21, 36
ladybugs 105
Lalymom 4, 21, 22, 39, 56, 68, 71, 87, 93, 110, 112
laundry basket 49
Lego 6, 43, 46, 52, 85
lemonade 70
letters see alphabet
lids 60, 83, 86
light table 53, 75
lion 13
Little Bins for Little Hands 5, 15, 18, 37, 38, 47, 52, 83, 85, 116, 119
locks 62
loom bands 110

M
marbles 20
math skills see numbers
maze 22, 47
measuring 12, 46, 60, 70, 87
mobile 95, 101
monsters 30
moon dust 50
moon rocks 89
muffin tin 48, 60
music 24, 76, 95

N
names 36, 56, 77, 79, 87
necklaces 33, 79
nest 14
numbers 15, 22, 28, 31, 40, 46, 47, 53, 77, 80, 81, 82, 83, 87, 114, 115
nuts 38

O
Oball 84
opening 60, 62, 66, 67, 69
Our Whimsical Days 5, 12, 20, 33, 51, 61, 65, 81, 86, 94, 97
owls 92

P
packing peanuts 10
painting 23, 25, 65, 100, 102, 103, 104, 105, 108, 109, 111, 120
paper plate 102, 111, 120
paper punch 16, 21, 32, 74, 92, 93, 96, 120
paperclips 28, 33
patterns 31, 32, 33, 36, 38, 78, 85, 97
peg doll 25, 50
pets 69
photos 16, 41
pincer grasp 10, 37, 38, 52, 60, 74, 80, 92, 98
pinch pots 99
pinching 13, 34, 54, 66, 87, 94, 99
pipe cleaners 38, 97, 101, 118
pipes, plastic 18
pipettes 83, 96, 105
plastic tubes 20
plastic eggs 113
plastic pipes 18
plastic tube shots 53
play dough 19, 37, 44, 52, 55, 87
pom poms 24, 49, 98, 109, 120
pool noodles 29, 81
pouches 60
pouring 46, 56, 61, 69, 70
powdered chalk 94
Powerful Mothering 4, 17, 23, 24, 35, 40, 57, 79, 88, 101, 104
Practical Life 59-71
pre-writing 45, 47, 50, 75
puffy paint 108
pumpkins 93, 115
puppets 16, 109

R
rainbow 17, 39, 84, 98, 111
resources 123
rolling 20, 24, 34, 37, 44, 87, 99

rolling pin 34
rubber bands 29

S
salt tray 45, 50
sand 51, 54, 56
scarves 84
School Time Snippets 5, 19, 31, 32, 49, 67, 77, 82, 99, 108, 120
science experiment 83
scissor skills 37, 60, 68, 93, 100, 112, 116, 120
scooping 46, 54, 56, 69, 114
Seasonal 107-121
Sensory 43-57
shakers 24
shapes 10, 21, 32, 35, 37, 45, 48, 53, 57, 74, 82, 87, 93, 96
shells 56, 105
shoebox 13, 66, 77, 115
shovels 56
shrinky dinks 21
slime 52
small world 19, 121
smashing 89
snacks 60, 67
snowman 121
sound 51
soup, sensory 46
spaghetti 102
spatial reasoning 13
spice container 67
spiders 55, 116
spray bottle 64, 78, 94
squeeze bottle 15
squeezing 15, 47, 60, 61, 64, 65, 76, 78, 83, 96, 102, 108, 114
squish bag 47
St Patricks's Day 111
stacking 17, 23, 51, 63, 81
stained glass 104
stickers 16, 22, 31, 77, 117, 120
Still Playing School 4, 16, 36, 55, 69, 70, 84, 100, 105, 109, 121
Stir The Wonder 5, 30, 48, 50, 63, 64, 78, 80, 89, 96, 117
strainer 36
straws 13, 37, 46, 100
structures see building
sun 102
symmetry 100

T
tape 66, 75
Thanksgiving 117
threading 36, 38, 79, 96, 97
tissue paper 15, 66, 112
tongs 48, 49, 80, 114
tools 12
toothbrush 71
toothpicks 10, 119, 121

towels 63
towers 17, 23, 34, 81
toy hammer 12, 89
Toys 9-25
tracing 88, 93, 112
trains 103
tripod grasp 38, 52, 119
turkey 117
tweezers 14, 47, 48, 49, 52, 80, 114, 115
twisting 22, 62, 67, 118

V
Valentine's Day 74, 83, 93, 110
Velcro 17, 30, 31, 62
vinegar 17, 64, 83
visual processing 15, 47

W
washers 38
washing 61, 64, 65
water beads 20
watercolor paint 45, 46, 96, 104, 105
web 116
whipped cream 57
wind chime 97
window clings 108
window washing 64
wrapping 34, 66, 95
wreath 120

Y
yarn 95, 96, 101

Z
zippers 67

Download printables here: https://goo.gl/tdsql6

TIME TO BRUSH!

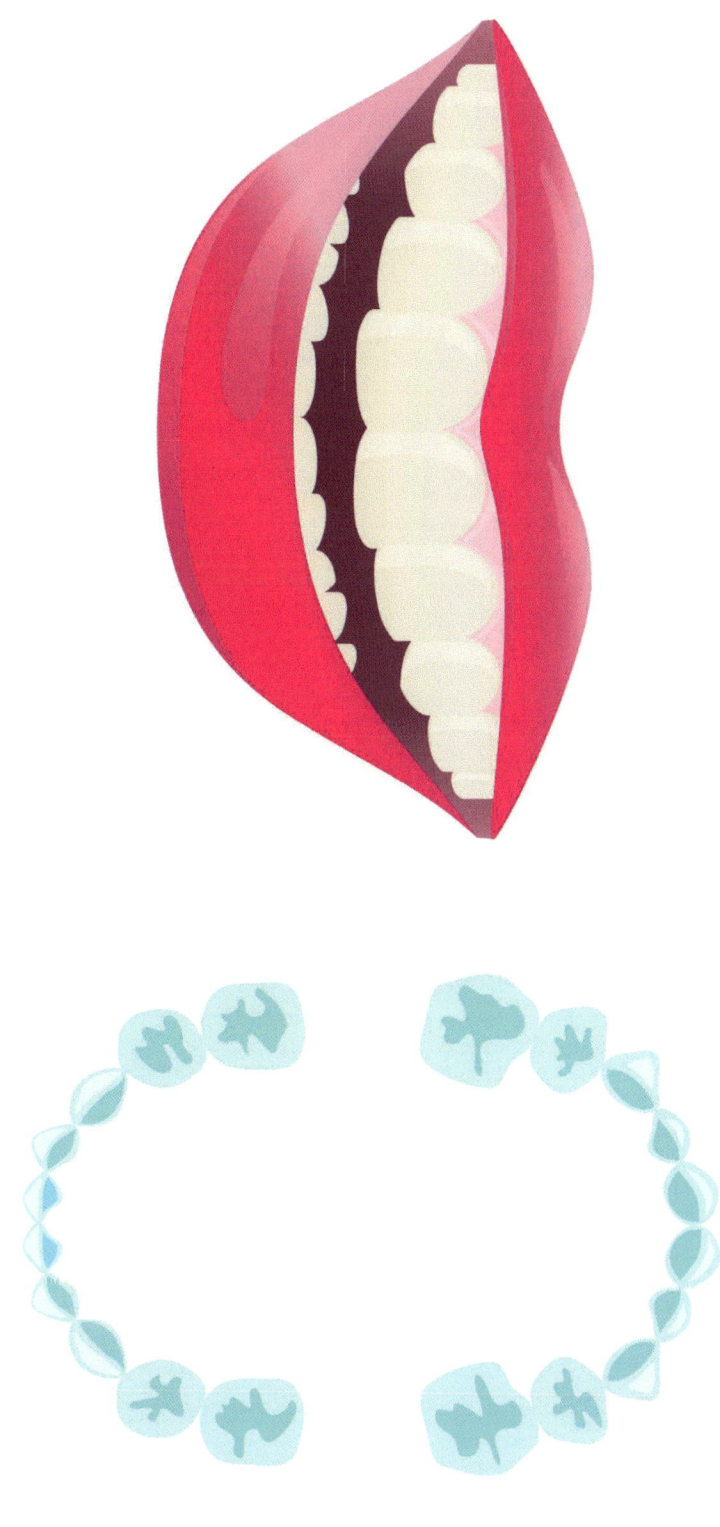

Directions: Insert this page into a page protector. Use dry erase markers or dry erase crayons to draw food on the teeth. Next, show your child how to use a spare toothbrush to brush the food off. Don't forget to get between the teeth!

This printable was created by Laura from Lalymom using clipart by Hidesy's Clipart with permission. All rights reserved.

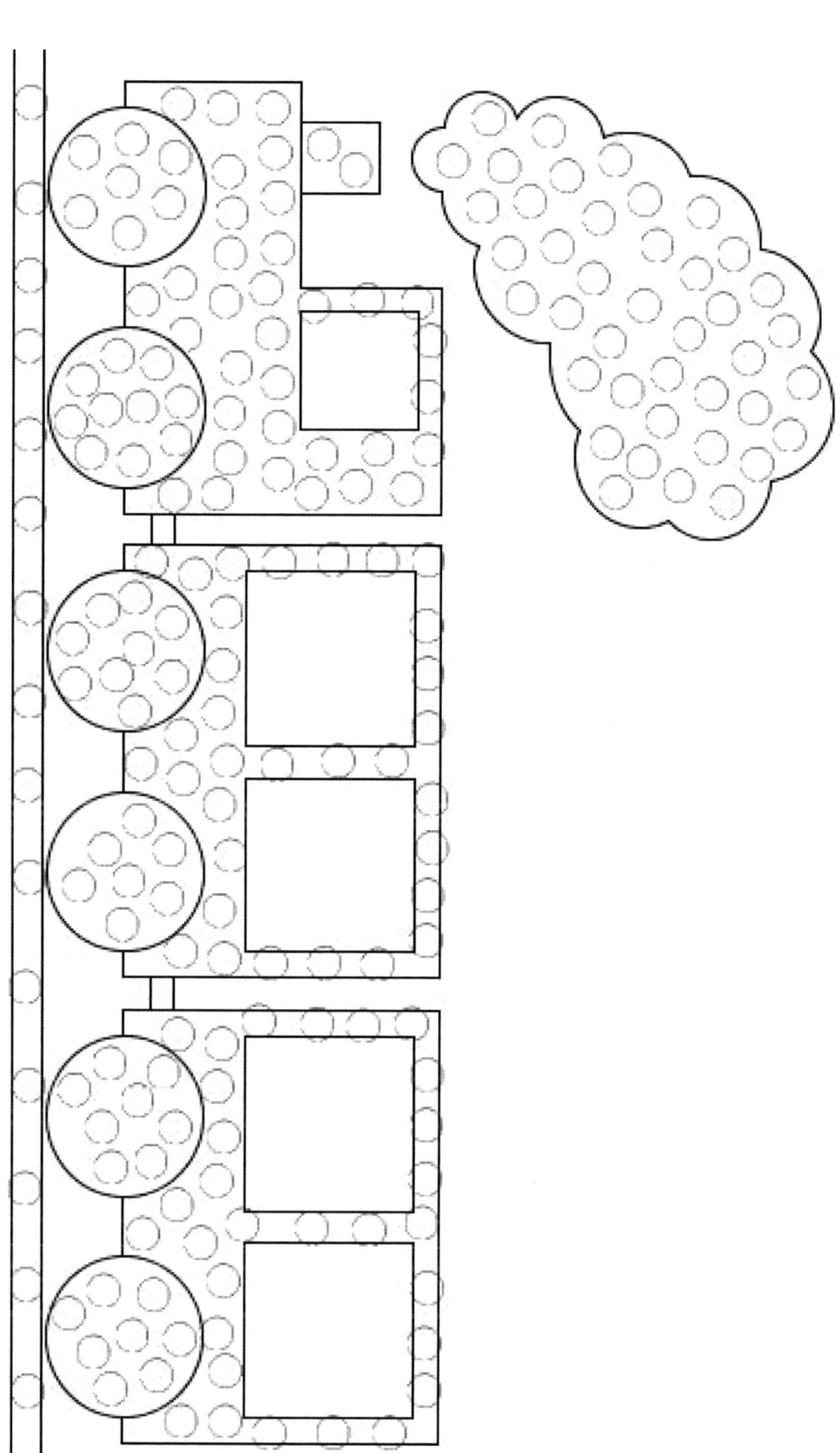
Q-Tip Steam Train from Craftulate.com
Personal use only

Template for Pom Pom Rainbow

Design-An-Egg Garland! Print this page, allow the ink to dry, then you are ready to create with your child!
1. Cut on the solid straight lines. 2. Fold on the dotted line and then continue folding the strip of paper, accordion style. 3. Cut the egg, cutting through all layers of paper, making sure that you allow the eggs to stay connected where the fold is. On each side. 4. Decorate and color!

Copyright Lalymom.com. All rights reserved. For personal and classroom use only. Do no sell or distribute.
Visit Lalymom.com for more fun!

www.finemotorideas.com

Printed in Great Britain
by Amazon